Technical Theatre &
Production Design:

In Immersive Theatre

Examining the Use of Theatrical Technologies in Creating an Immersive Micro-Scene

About the Author

Kieran Burgess has worked in UK and Singapore theatres in a range of technical and design roles, including staging, set, lighting, sound and stage and production management. He has been involved in the creative process of a number of original productions, before moving into the education sector as a teacher of Production Arts. Whilst teaching the technicians and designers of tomorrow, Kieran devised several original experiences for audiences, and developed an interest for immersive theatre in particular. He continues to teach, though also teaches Acting, Drama and Theatre Studies more generally. Teaching Drama internationally has enabled him to fully appreciate the needs and requirements of students embarked on IB Theatre, A-Level and GCSE courses, and holds a keen interest in providing relevant and challenging research material and learning experiences for them. Despite also taking on acting and directing roles, Kieran is still happiest when manipulating theatre technology to express an artistic interpretation. Away from theatre, he repeats his love for the clash of art and technology with a keen pursuit of photography, and sells photographs in print form.

EXAMINING THE USE OF THEATRICAL TECHNOLOGIES IN AN IMMERSIVE MICRO-SCENE

Third Edition

ISBN: 9781679513343

First Published in Great Britain in 2013.
This Edition Published 2020.
Copyright © Kieran Burgess 2013.

Acknowledgements

The project that is the foundation of this book could not have happened without significant support of a number of people. I would very much like to record my thanks and gratitude to the students of the 2013 Production Arts class: Danny, Izzy, Jo, Kieran, Rosaria and Sam - who acted as crew, and thoroughly deserved their Distinction grades. To Brian Gorrie, whose unwavering willingness to get his hands dirty was second only to his expert knowledge of sound design and cueing software. To Helen Breheny, Anna McVeigh and Jack Ryan, whose precious spare time was given over to creating performances beyond their years. To Kim and Eddie for never questioning why the studio was such a mess. To Meic Watkins for reading a few too many drafts of this, and for a few practical theatrical tips along the way. And to my long-suffering wife, Ali, who just wanted to go home before dark.

Kieran

Third Edition Update:

I'd like to add my thanks to all those who previously bought a copy of this book, and to you who bought this copy. I truly did not expect to sell more than one or two copies - and those only to my family who felt obliged. But I have been both pleasantly surprised and pushed into action to improve the niggles that I saw in the last edition as a result of the unexpected popularity of the publication. This edition, therefore, tidies up some of those issues I had discovered only after the paperback edition went live - mostly formatting and aesthetics.

New discoveries continue to be made in the field of Immersive Theatre, and my own practice has broadened to Scenography as a collaborator more generally in theatre. Such findings are not appropriate for this book, with its case-study model, so you can expect to find those in my next book already underway and due for publication soon.

Kieran

Preface

Immersive design is found in a range of contexts: immersive theatre production; static installation art; theme park attractions; and museum exhibits, to name a few. Here, we introduce the Micro-Scene as a device to explore the use of scenography and theatrical technology within a short piece of immersive theatre. This book focuses on a research project carried out during 2011 and 2012 in Manchester, UK. A production, entitled *9/11*, immersed participants in Manhattan on the morning of September 11, 2001, shortly after the first World Trade Centre tower collapsed. *9/11* drew on observations of immersive design in practice, and reviews published theory within the field of scenography. An illusionistic street environment was produced: real bricks in buildings; sandstone walls; broken glass on the floor; with all major senses catered for in an attempt to suggest an experience of being in the vicinity of the twin tower attacks.

Technical theatre has grown during my lifetime alone from being a fringe of theatre; the dark corners in which artistic endeavour is converted into a series of logic, numbers, lengths and widths, and measurable waveforms; from the functional - to a huge field of design, artistry and exploration in its own right. Such is the broad spectrum of research within the design departments of technical theatre, that sound, light and scenography students can spend their lives developing knowledge in just one genre of theatre. And that is before we consider the knowledge and research that is necessary to develop the technical, functional departments of the discipline. We now have students at high schools and colleges in the UK, who take public examinations in no subject other than technical theatre (sometimes called Production Arts). The Higher Education sector is growing ever stronger, with courses for lighting technicians, sound technicians, stage managers, lighting designers, sound designers, set designers and every combination thereof. Even traditional Drama courses are seeing the need to cater for the growing interest in technical theatre and production design: GCSE, A-Level, International Baccalaureate and BTEC courses all require or support students who choose to study the disciplines within production.

This book explores how technical theatre - both artistic design and technical functionality - can be used both generally, and also specifically within the field of immersive theatre. It explores the notions of interactivity and engagement from a production point of view: we know that production design and theatrical technologies can add significant value to a piece of immersive theatre, but can they replace actors? Can we immerse audiences into a world not of their own, only or primarily using technology? This book will focus on the research project, *9/11,* in order to attempt to answer these questions. The research, trials, experiments (both successful and unsuccessful), build process and shaping of final performances are included here. This book does not claim to offer the perfect Micro-Scene by any means - areas for improvement are acknowledged. However it does include honest observations not only on the use of the use of modern theatrical technologies, but on the artistic journey, the devising process and the on coping with limitations of budget, space and personnel.

Introduction

Immersive design is visible as a significant feature of various art forms. Notably used in performances by immersive theatre companies, such as Punchdrunk (http://www.punchdrunk.org.uk) and Slung Low (http://web.me.com/slung.low - both since 2000), immersive design aims to engage participants into an environment that supports the intentions of the producer. Theatrical performances offer a driven narrative, in which audiences are sometimes included as participants (for example, Slung Low's They Only Come At Night: Resurrections, 2009). Alternatively, immersive design in theatre has also been used to support a site-specific performance, where audiences are not required to interact with actors or narrative (for example, Slung Low's Helium, 2008).

Outside of theatre, immersive design exists to provide experiences for participants with or without a driven narrative. 'Museum Theatre' is a rapidly growing area (Tolkoff, 1995), which places characters into another place and/or time, with the aim of educating and engaging visitors. One such example is the Imperial War Museum North, Salford. Here, the life of a working woman during World War II is presented via a costumed character delivering a monologue to bystanders (2012, http://www.iwm.org.uk). She is surrounded by props and artefacts from her time, although total immersion is not possible due to the open nature of the performance space, and the wider museum environment beyond. 'Total Immersion' is a term coined by Ilya and Emilia Kabakov to describe their fine art installations (2012, website section: 'Interactive Installation'). Total immersion uses purely scenographic elements (hard scenery, props, visual imagery, along with lighting and sound) to create a world into which participants enter, though the absence of actors or a moving narrative means that participants enter into a snapshot in time rather than into a moving narrative. Immersive environments are created in other non-theatre contexts, where immersive design methods are used in theme parks, usually on a grand scale. Attractions such as Alton Towers and Blackpool Pleasure Beach use immersive design to set particular rides into particular locations (the Haunted House at both theme parks are useful examples). Universal Studios Singapore takes the principle of building impressive stage sets one step further: for their Halloween special event, the park offers a number of large-scale immersive environments. One such scene sees a full-sized crashed helicopter placed onto the realistic and full-sized New York multi-street set, adding actors in full costume and blood-effect make-up to roam around the area, interacting with visitors and using dialogue and props to suggest they are contaminated with some incurable lab-engineered disease. It is whilst discussing the application of scenographic skills to the world of theme park attractions, that Michael Devine, creator of many theme park environments, observes that the intention of immersive design is to "put the participant in a place not of their world." (cited in Ludwig, 2011: 54). It is this intention that defines immersive design across all art forms; from the immersive theatre production that aims to offer audiences an experience of being in the world of their characters, to the installation artist whose 'place not of [the participants'] world' may be on a more intellectual and possibly symbolic level than the face-value thrills and awe of Devine's Disneyland sets.

Frank Ludwig expands on Devine's explanation of the objective of the immersive design process:

> *"The objective...is not to create an environment that supports the telling of a story, but to design an experience of a story being told...first, concern for the experience of the audience is brought to the forefront. Second, the story is not the end itself, but a means by which the experience is rendered meaningful." (2011: 55)*

The most important aspect of immersive design according to Devine is to place participants in another world, whereas according to Ludwig, it is the experience that this other world contributes to that is paramount. This book aims to draw on observations of the use of immersive design across theatre, museum education, theme parks and fine art, and examine the success or otherwise of using theatrical technologies to be the driving force in providing an experience for participants. To do this, a short, self-contained experience that I call a Micro-Scene, was created. Primarily, this research is investigating the use of theatre technologies in a Micro-Scene, particularly whether a range of technologies combined can be a focus within the field of immersive theatre.

The exploration of these questions is still ongoing: I cannot claim to have found definitive answers to all questions arising, though areas for further research are clearly identified in the latter stages of this book, once evidence and outcomes have been discussed. As a work in progress, it was decided that a snapshot of research should be formed into a milestone practical experiment.

This experiment is a Micro-Scene that I created, entitled 9/11.

9/11 is set in the immediate aftermath of the attacks on New York City on September 11th 2001, and primarily revolves around a street corner. Audiences are given this location and timing information via 'live' TV news coverage shown passively in the front of house area (see accompanying video appendices A and B), before being placed in the street. Here, participants are free to explore a dust-filled environment (caused, as the audience discover via the news reports before entering the street, by the first tower collapsing), with building facades and interiors, rubble and building detritus and warped street furniture. A small television inside a deli continues to show the live news coverage of what is going on a couple of blocks away, the sound audible through the smashed windows. Sounds of nearby sirens, shouting, walkie-talkie chatter and the occasional crunch of a body landing on the ground can be heard from several directions. Broken glass crunches underfoot (Video Appendix D, from 00:12s), and hundreds of sheets of paper litter the streets - some still smouldering. The air is still heavy with smoke and concrete dust, and visibility is limited. The smell of burning is powerful, and the taste of the dust is noticeable. Participants meet characters, who see them and converse with them, and in one case show them footage they filmed that morning on their handheld camera (Video Appendix C), before a soundscape (Video Appendix D, between 10:50 and 16:20) and projection remove the audience from the location and present them with a more passive telling of the firefighters' story. This prepares audiences for a reflective zone; adjacent to the street but not theatricalised, except some gentle lighting and a static word art projection. This zone houses written accounts by survivors, newspaper front pages, missing posters and the projected 'Wordle' word art (Appendix A), along with a large space on the wall on which audiences can read other participants' accounts of where they were when they heard the news, and add their own. They are free to leave this zone, and thus the entire experience, whenever they wish. There was no further persuasion or instruction - characters did not remain in this space and a door to the corridor outside was left open. The street zone and the reflective zone is shown from a participant's point of view, in its entirety, in Video Appendix D.

Research Methodology

The *9/11* project was the major experiment within the research phase, although it is worth mentioning that the performance was a milestone in a longer discovery process, rather than a summation of learning. Research was centred around the practical processes and experiences, drawing on Robin Nelson's triangulation model for practice-as-research in the performing arts (Nelson, 2006: 114). With *9/11* as the 'product' in the centre of Nelson's model, the process began with observations and analysis of immersive design concepts as used by other practitioners. Coupled with a literary review into theoretical frameworks of elements of lighting, sound, scenography and immersive theatre, this observation of others' work forms the corner of the triangle that Nelson calls, 'conceptual framework' (ibid.: 114). He explains innovative practice as being, "informed by theoretical perspectives, either new in themselves, or perhaps newly explored in a given medium" (ibid.: 114). Throughout this book, I will refer both to theoretical knowledge applied in their original contexts, and to those applied across art forms and genres (that is, not in their original context).

In planning and producing the product of *9/11*, prior experience of working across a variety of genres in commercial theatre and theatre within education was drawn upon. This tacit knowledge was key to using time and resources efficiently, and was applied consciously and subconsciously - a problem acknowledged by Nelson (ibid.: 113). With the awareness that such embedded 'know-how' is in danger of not being documented, details of construction and plans that were naturally created in the process of production are included, and each is referred to within appropriate sections of this book. Following Nelson's advice, the existence of the product is documented, along with elements of the creation process, through photographs and video recordings, some of which are included or referred to throughout.

The third corner of Nelson's model acknowledges that:

"nobody works in a vacuum; all creative work operates within - or reacts against - established discourses." (ibid.: 114)

Critical reflection has been an ongoing concern throughout this research. Though this book in itself is a major reflective component, and concluding sections are the most critical within it, it was necessary to reflect at every stage. Herein, reference is made to several instances where a number of methods were tried, reflected on and changed before the final performance, as well as a number of areas that made it to the end of the project before reflection deemed them unsuccessful. Nelson refers to the documenting of audience responses as a useful way of, "making the tacit more explicit" (ibid.: 113), and whilst audience responses were garnered, mostly throughout the latter stages of the project, it is somewhat regretful that these were not documented formally by way of video recording or questionnaire.

Process

In this section, I will describe the various scenographic elements and production techniques used in 9/11, and explain why they were used above other methods in order to achieve the end product.

Available Resources

The venue that housed the 9/11 experiment is a black box studio space in a sixth form college in Manchester. The space contains operable walls, which can be positioned so as to separate an auditorium with raked bleacher seating from a flat stage area, with a useable playing area measuring approximately ten metres by five metres. A detailed description of the technical equipment available can be seen at Appendix I.

Conditional to the use of the space and students for this research, I was obliged by the school management to offer several opportunities to school students through the design of this project. I was also obliged to provide a piece of finished theatre that could be accessed by students across the school - from age eleven to eighteen. These conditions, as well as my desire to provide a meaningful piece of theatre for all ages, contributed to the shaping of the target audience for 9/11. For adults who vividly remember watching the story unfold, it was to be a fresh angle, looking at the very personal impact of the attacks. However, this piece was also designed to inform and educate current school pupils who weren't born in 2001, or were too young to remember: for this group, 9/11 was to be their first direct encounter with the events that the rest of us know so much about, thanks to 24 hour news channels. The content has therefore been created with both groups in mind. In order to further explore the educational benefits of this project, the design and build itself was an assessed project for a group of sixth form Production Arts students. These sixth formers were studying lighting, sound and stage management, and work full time on the production of shows in the space. The whole planning and build process included them, through production meetings and workshops. The development of new skills, and the application and adaptation of existing knowledge, was a learning experience for these students. Using a small number of GCSE Drama students to provide the characters within the scene also provided opportunities to explore immersive theatre - a genre certainly not attempted in their school previously. For the two groups of students however, the element of the project brief that looked to its purpose as an educational tool was extended far beyond the reach of the final product. For these students, the extensive planning and research - either into the scene being reproduced (based on real photographs and real streets) or the stories of those involved - has massively increased their knowledge and understanding of the events of the day. Ultimately, their emotional response to the individuals they have met through the creation of 9/11 has been formed through the development of the show, rather than simply the end product as found by the audience. So, to follow through to a logical conclusion, for these students; if their understanding and empathy has been expanded from beginning the project, rather than just the final piece of theatre, then the show for them has so far been eight months long, and has not been confined to the actual theatre space.

Finally, it should be noted that whilst resources were strong in terms of available production labour, and in terms of the infrastructure and major equipment in the theatre space, there was no budget available for this show. Wherever possible, 9/11 had to use existing resources, only purchasing necessary items, such as consumables, out of the box office fund (containing the profit from previous shows). This meant spending was closely monitored, and could not exceed £150 without the risk of the project being discontinued.

The Participants' Journey

The first decision to be made was the journey through which an audience would travel. The specific scenic elements, and the placing of those elements could not be designed or built until the journey of the participants was established. The question was asked: what events will participants encounter? Appendix C shows the initial proposal, which included front of house 'live' TV news coverage, female university students with portable footage from their own camera that morning, a man emerging from the World Trade Centre buildings and a possible police officer ordering the evacuation of the audience from the street scene, to go with police radio noise. At this point, there was no intention to create the reflective zone that audiences were eventually ushered into. Already at the first proposed narrative plan, it was intended that the university students (referred to as the NYU Dorm Girls on the plan) would emerge from a deli or diner. This building was intended to be big enough for audiences to enter and explore. The other side of the street would be dominated by the facade of an office building, whilst the furthest point from the audience's entrance would be closed off by a pile of rubble. I will go into further detail about the reasoning behind the inclusion of these scenic elements later, but for now it should be pointed out that their inclusion at such an early stage was vital in 'cordoning off' the backstage areas of the space, without detracting from the world that participants were placed in. This early plan also included a fire hydrant; which played no part in driving the narrative, but demonstrated an early intention to suggest the illusion of a street scene.

As the plans progressed, elements of the narrative were changed. The NYU girls were retained, and used the deli to hide from the first collapsing tower, but there was less focus on inviting audience into the deli, instead bringing action into the street scene so that budgetary constraints affecting the interior of the deli did not detract from the desired illusion. The man entering the scene from the World Trade Centre buildings was removed from the latter versions of the show, and replaced with a young man on the phone to his girlfriend in the remaining tower. The police radio noise and police officer were mostly removed from the final version, to be replaced with 'the firefighters' story': fire department radio transmissions with the story of one such firefighter projected onto a black wall. Whilst the live actor portraying a police officer was removed, there remained an offstage police officer, ordering the evacuation of the area via loudhailers.

The narrative plans went through various minor amendments, and one major amendment before arriving at the version used for final audiences in May 2012. The major amendment can be found in Appendix D, and the 'final' version can be seen in Appendix E. With a clear plan for the unfolding narrative before an audience, more detailed plans for the various elements of set required could be formulated.

The whole experience is broken down into three zones: The first zone is the front of house area, with the live news coverage. The second zone is a street scene, in the vicinity of the World Trade Centre, but not directly underneath. The third zone is referred to here as the reflective zone. The final set consisted of the following elements:

- •Buildings
  - •A delicatessen, with interior (figure 1)
  - •The corner of an office building (figure 2)

•A substantial pile of rubble and detritus seemingly caused by the collapse of a building nearby, but not immediately overhead (visible in figures 3 and 4)
•Street Furniture
  •Metal posts holding street name signs (figure 4)
  •Fire hydrant (figure 5)
  •Overhead operational traffic lights (figure 6)
  •Overhead Direction sign ('Battery Pk'), as intended for drivers (visible in figure 4)
  •A raised pavement (visible in figure 3)
•A continuation of the street, projected on to a cyclorama behind the rubble
•A floor completely covered in pulverised concrete, pieces of paper, broken glass and smouldering matter from the initial aircraft impact and subsequent collapse
•Plain black flats and drapes at the perimeter of the space
•A reflective zone

•Museum-like display boards, containing contemporary written and visual accounts

•Projected word art

•A large area of paper on which to write own experiences

Figure 1

Figure 2

Figure 3

Figure 4

Figure 5

Figure 6

Figure 8

Figure 9

Set

The overriding aim of the street set was to provide participants with a multi-sensory illusion of being caught up in the disaster. The street scene, being the key area of the experience, was intended to create a strong impact on audiences. Referring to Devine's 'other world', it was necessary to give audiences an environment that they would not expect to see inside a drama studio or education facility. Indeed, Devine elaborates on his 'other world' theory, when discussing his intentions throughout the design process at Tokyo DisneySea Theme Park:

"When you enter the environment you are in a world totally separated from the mass and heave of daily life in Tokyo...Our collective intent was to wipe away the visitor's sense of the everyday." (cited in Ludwig, 2011: 54)

Building a moderately large-scale outdoors location in detail is one method of providing a completely opposite space to the one participants expect to find on entering the room. For ease, this desired impact was referred to as the 'wow factor' throughout the production process. Punchdrunk theatre company are a useful source in judging the impact of this 'wow factor'. In It Felt Like a Kiss, at the Manchester International Festival in 2009, Punchdrunk theatre company included what The Guardian called a "meticulous recreation of period suburban America" (2009: unpaged). This set included an exterior location, with neatly-trimmed lawns and picket fences - which, when placed within an indoor setting, does hold the ability to impress an audience. The BBC review of the show points out that,

"Visitors are encouraged to scrutinise every prop in this unscripted thriller. There's a lot to investigate and I become engrossed in books, photographs and letters," (Price, 2009: unpaged).

This sense of free will to explore a scene is a consideration for what a Micro-Scene should be.

Littering a set with props that can be investigated and interacted with can immediately enhance the immersive experience for audiences, and is an example of how naturally-occurring interaction (naturally within the confines of a created piece of theatre) leads to deeper immersion, which in turn leads to greater engagement (the relationship between interaction and immersion, and their relevance to the Micro-Scene, is discussed in more detail later). Though this is merely one method of immersing an audience within a scene, it is a method that is very appealing to the idea of what the Micro-Scene should become. The other element of It Felt Like a Kiss that influenced 9/11 is the recreation of the outdoors, indoors. By entering an indoor space and suddenly finding objects and materials that one would only associate with the outdoors, this Punchdrunk set is a clear example of Devine's aim of placing audiences into another world. The same set in a large outdoor lot would not hold the same 'wow factor'.

Alan Lane, creative director of Slung Low, shares his thoughts on immersive environments, generally:

"We put the audience into the middle of a film, except that it's real, it's 3D, you can touch it, and if there's water you'll get wet, because water is wet. It's where you can look behind you, in front of you, above you and below you and there will be the world we create." (cited in London Theatre Blog website, 2009: unpaged)

The idea that theatre can also use the sense of touch when communicating with the audience is a concept that goes hand in hand with the intentions of immersive theatre: an audience can never be truly immersed in an environment where they can not wholly engage or interact with their surroundings. Traditional theatre, in the mainstream, uses sight and sound only. By utilising touch (and perhaps smell and taste), the micro-scene can go a long way to distinguishing itself as an extension of the traditional theatre techniques, and to qualifying as a truly immersive environment. Lane also discusses the free will to look all around, and to find the created 'other world' at all angles. The premise that the audience have the free will, or at least the illusion of free will to explore their environment, to look all around them and see the world the author wants them to see, is a strong defining characteristic of immersive design.

The two buildings on the street set served multiple purposes. In the formative stages of the narrative and set design, it became clear that devices would need to be created to keep the audience from going into areas they weren't supposed to. However, the necessity to block access to backstage undressed and unlit areas conflicted with the desire to maintain a sense of free will amongst participants. By using buildings, a physical barrier was provided that also blocked sight to the expanse of the cyclorama (the use of which will be explained later on), and prevented access to the offstage area to the right of the office. The reason for these barriers being building frontages was to aid the audience in identifying the location as a street.

The first building to be confirmed in the plans was the delicatessen. The structure of the building was provided by canvas flats, with the visible corner being two flats hinged together into a book (see figure 7). This joint needed work to close this hinged gap and retain the look of a brick and stone building. This was done by firstly dressing the corner with a piece of plastic downspout from the exterior of a local building. The bottom of the pipe was snapped off, to suggest damage from flying debris. To cover the remainder of this joint, a novel technique was employed: folding a piece of paper into a pentahedron and slotting it within the gap, then applying decorator's caulk over the gaps and painting over the whole section, allowed for seamless smoothing with the book flat, and subsequent blending of paint. A real deli in lower Manhattan was found on the internet, with their sign and name copied for authenticity. In order to meet the needs of the production whilst also spending almost no money, some frugal stagecraft was employed. The sign was made by painting 3mm plywood with the background colour, and then printing out the letters onto A3 paper, cutting and gluing each letter into position. This was done so as to ensure straight and uniform letters, and avoid the 'home-made' look from painting letters directly onto the ply.

Some letters were deliberately peeled slightly off the plywood, and some darker paint applied to corners, to give the weathered look. A key feature of the deli structure was the brick on its main wall (facing the street). In order to make 9/11 a truly multi-sensory piece of theatre, it was decided that wherever possible, Alan Lane's concept of an audience being able to touch and feel what is around them should be followed: by creating a multi-sensory environment, the aim was to further increase the degree of immersion, thus hoping for greater engagement. Whilst standard methods of creating brick effect walls in theatre were reviewed (from two-dimensional painted bricks, to polystyrene, to fibre-reinforced plastic and latex), the ultimate decision was to use real bricks to give the deli real authenticity. Polystyrene, moulded plastic and latex can offer an authentic look of brickwork from an auditorium, but the illusion is soon vanished when an audience member looks closely, or touches the wall. The real brick wall offered a sense of permanence that is associated with 'real' buildings outdoors, and was intended to aid the desired 'wow factor' of walking into a space that immediately removed the audience from the actual location of a college building. Of course, this brick wall could not be permanent, so mortar could not be used. Instead, cardboard spacers were inserted between rows, and between individual bricks, to create the gap naturally found with genuine brick walls. This method allowed for a smooth and efficient removal of the wall when the time to strike the set arrived. Other elements of the deli included: brightly painted walls, though distressed with mud and grit from outside; small plant pots that had fallen off the window sill, and; colourful ribbon streamers across the main entrance. It was intended that these bright colours and plant life would juxtapose against the debris and destruction, with the vitality of the plants on the floor, amongst broken glass, ash and concrete dust intended to offer a subtle contrast at this height. The deli was originally intended to be a feature that included a large interior, that an audience could enter and explore. It was thus necessary to include wide windows to invite participants' curiosity. The window frames were cut out of the canvas flats, and reveals and window sills applied to add the third dimension to otherwise flat walls. Because of these wide windows, it was necessary to also create an interior to the deli. Whilst this was mostly dressing; cups, plates, half-eaten food, cash register, posters and knick-knacks on the wall; a small television was placed on one counter to provide visuals and audio of a 'live' TV news channel reporting what was happening round the corner at the World Trade Centre. The television was fitted with a (fake) antenna protruding from it to reinforce the suggestion that it was live television, though the media was actually played back from a DVD player secreted underneath the counter. This television set inside the deli was important in tying the Front of House TV news area with the street scene, as well as anchoring the continuous time passage convention (the day began at approximately 8.20am in the front of house area, and continued in 'real time' throughout the pre-show zone and into the street). The ongoing news footage also served to further contextualise the street scene and its contents. The audio from the interior television meant that the window frames could not be filled with glass. Instead, I decided to create the effect of blown out windows, which apart from a striking visual element, would help to create a multi-sensory effect of devastation on the floor, an area that I will return to later. Jagged pieces of window were glued into the window frames, though the practicalities of encouraging participants to explore and touch the set meant that glass had to be replaced with perspex for this job; placed at ideal hand height, and therefore essential to use safe material.

During the latter stages of planning, it was apparent that budget restrictions would not allow the build of a deli interior detailed enough to withstand the scrutiny of participants inside it. Simply double-siding flats would not give the required depth in the walls, and the building of another set of flats, and indeed a roof, to provide an interior was too costly. There was also the added concern over the amount of space remaining on the street itself; had the deli been large enough to accommodate audiences entering, the 'outside' space would have not been wide enough to accurately pass off as a street or path. The deli became smaller, and inadmissible to audiences, though in the interests of maintaining the illusion of free will there were no physical barriers. By keeping the interior dark, except for the television set, and the doorway covered in streamers, no audiences attempted to enter.

The other building in the street was the side of an office building, disappearing off stage behind black drapes. The corner of the building was visible, roughly opposite the corner of the deli, adding to the impression of a road intersecting the smaller passage that the audience entered into. Again created using flats, there was a structural difference required between the two buildings. Whereas the deli flats did not need to take extra weight of any significance (the brick wall facade was freestanding in front of the flats), the office building was covered in a sandstone effect that added considerable weight to the structure. Due to budget limitations, only four new flats could be constructed. I decided to build hard, ply-covered timber flats and double-sided for extra strength, with two of these flats positioned at either end of the building and hinged together into two book flats. This harder, stronger material was then able to take the weight of the sandstone mixture, as well as provide a firmer grip for it to stick. The canvas flats (drawn from existing stock) in the middle of the building

were unable to hold the sticky sandstone
mixture, and so were covered in posters for
bands and concerts taken from genuine New
York-based promoters' websites, in order to hide
the difference across the wall. The sandstone
mixture was made using several experiments,
eventually settling on a mix of road grit, white
paint, unibond (a PVA glue and water mixture)
and pure PVA glue for the application. This
mixture, when dried, provided a highly authentic
look and feel of sandstone, and due to its careful
placement, gave the impression that the whole
building was made of this. Whilst papier-mâché
or pulped cardboard would have given a similar
visual effect (useful for end-on format theatre),
it was the impact on a participant created when
they touch the wall and find it feels just like
sandstone that was important, even matching
properties such as the slight coming away of a
few grains of sand when running fingers over it.
Applying the sandstone mix was, however, quite
time consuming, as it could only be done by
hand in small amounts. The amount of visible
sandstone was therefore kept to a minimum. The
top half of the office building was covered in
poly insulation board, carved and painted to look

like slabs of grey stone bricks, and glued to both the hard flats and the canvas. As it was intended to be out of reach, it was necessary only to provide visually accurate material, and not to be accurate to the touch, but one enterprising tall participant did manage to feel this material: perhaps placing this section higher would have prevented the break in suspension of disbelief here.

The primary function of the office building initially was to hide the section of cyclorama that wasn't being used, and the backstage areas beyond it. It was therefore unnecessary to provide any real depth to it, or windows and doors. It did, however, hold a secondary function; which was to house the Deputy Stage Manager and her communications console (cue light only due to her proximity to the audience). A projector and operator was also housed behind this building, with the aperture for the projector needing to be minimised as much as possible. To keep the projector and its opening through the poly bricks of the flats as low-key as possible, a piece of gauze was initially stretched across the small cut-out, and painted to match the surrounding grey stone bricks. However, the relatively low power lamp in the projector was not powerful enough to shine through this gauze onto the opposite black wall, and retain enough clarity on the images. The gauze was removed, and a larger window created near to the actual aperture, with window sill and frames, and broken glass around and beneath it. The aim of this larger window - very much out of audience's reach to look through - was to distract attention from the smaller projection aperture, and to give the impression that the smaller hole was simply another small service window.

Beyond the office building was a large pile of rubble, containing stone, brick, glass and recognisable parts of buildings such as beams, twisted metal and ceiling tiles. The practical reason for its inclusion was to restrict access to the cyclorama (which had an image of the street continuing on back projected onto it; I will go into more detail about this later) and the offstage areas of the far end of the space. Artistically, the pile of rubble was large enough to be a significant feature to audiences entering, and immediately created the impression of destruction. To build such a large pile of rubble, some theatrical 'cheating' took place: rostra was built at staggered heights in the corner of the space, with irregular shapes being highest at the cyclorama, and tapering down to floor level further into the street. A large beige floorcloth was then draped over the rostra (the colour to blend well with the eventual dust and ash used over the whole space) and the detritus placed on top. This tiered rostra then helped to suggest that the pile of rubble was actually much more substantial that it really was, planting the seed that destruction in the area was large-scale.

Protruding through the rubble was a red fire-hydrant (figure 3) - similar in design to those seen on U.S. Films and TV shows, thus playing on the image that audiences are assumed to have of a street location in New York. The hydrant was also originally intended to be a focal point during the "firefighters' story" section, with the bright red contrasting well with the beige-grey dust and ash surrounding, but later experiments suggested the focus on a walkie-talkie to be more poignant. A metal post with the names of the two streets intersecting at the office building and deli also protruded from the rubble, twisted and leaning heavily as though impacted by the force of the rubble around it. The street signs on the pole were made by printing out the names of the two streets in the same font used for the genuine article, and gluing them to pieces of cut perspex. These hard signs were then attached to the pole using jubilee clips, as found on real street signs. A raised pavement, using rostra, ran alongside the office building; a subtle element to reinforce the idea that this location is outdoors.

Overhead, a large canvas flat was painted with a similar shade of green found on American road signs, and the correct font was found and used to print off each letter of 'Battery Pk', with an arrow below and a route number above - a direct copy of an actual road sign hanging above West Street in lower Manhattan. The detail was accurate enough to ensure that even the white border around the edge of the sign was replicated, however this sign was hung from a tab track using steel wire, rather than from a metal cylinder as found over roads, due to the constraints of being indoors. This sign was included not only to add to the sense of outdoors, but to help the audience place themselves within the scene: it told the audience that the space that was blocked by the rubble, and that led into the projected image on the cyclorama, was a main road.

The final piece of street furniture was the overhanging traffic signal. First thoughts were to buy a real traffic signal, in order to support the illusion of being in a 'working' street scene. However, acquiring a yellow (American) product would cost in the region of £200 plus postage from the U.S. - more than the total budget for the whole show. The next stage was to make it in-house. Originally, the intention was for this box to be manufactured using glossy yellow plastic, to give the same finish as the metal casings found on American traffic signals. Experimentations with plastic cement and strip heaters to bend the plastic into rounded corners, ended with the conclusion that once complete, the joints would not hold the weight of the lighting fixtures that would go inside the box. The end product was constructed of an MDF box, with O-rings and ply visors for the lamp faces cut using CAD software linked to a precision cutting tool. Three LED Chroma Q fixtures were bolted inside the box to provide the illumination, the importance being on fixtures that could be controlled via DMX from the lighting desk. With DMX and power cables exiting the box through a hole cut out of the top, and a hanging point bolted through the top adjacent to this hole and reinforced inside with steel brackets, the entire practical prop was suspended using steel cable from the truss.

Finally, garden spiders were introduced to the various items of street furniture, where they spun webs that not only helped to reinforce the 'outdoors' illusion, but also added subtle undertones of desertion and abandonment: sufficiently subtle to reinforce the eeriness of the scene without being obviously out of place.

In order to bed the buildings and street furniture in to a wider environment, the portion of cyclorama behind the rubble was filled with an image of a street in lower Manhattan covered in debris, with smashed windows and smoke filling the air. This was included so as to give the illusion that the destruction constructed in the main space continued down the street, as well as giving clear indication to audiences that this was a major street intersection. The 'Battery Pk' road sign hung above this image, pointing the way down the projected road. In the final performances, the image was 'blended' with the rest of the set by filling the space with smoke and haze. This limited visibility not only matched the smokiness of the image being projected, but provided the subtlety required to prevent this projection from standing out. The limited visibility of the road and buildings projected behind the rubble also added to the illusion, as the audience were given the impression of being in an area where one of the World Trade Centre towers had recently collapsed. The decision-making process, and details of the various experimental stages of this projection are detailed below, in the section on visual media.

It was decided that the street scene was to be the main experiment in creating a version of Michael Devine's 'other world'. Although a piece of theatre was created, it was intended that the audience should not find this fact particularly highlighted, in order to suspend disbelief and become immersed and engaged into the environment. It was imperative, therefore, that no scenic element was included that would be immediately obvious as not being of the 'other world'. With the budgetary and resource limitations present throughout this experiment, it was simply not possible to accurately create an entire New York street, across every degree, within the space. The rule was devised and applied from an early stage that, for this street scene, where an accurate element could not be created, it was to be left blank. Wendall Harrington summarised the underlying theory succinctly, when she claims that,

"The elements that are projected by the audience are far more interesting than anything I can project." (cited in Barbour, 2011: 31).

Here she considers audience imagination to be more powerful than the imagery imposed upon participants by authors. With theatrical convention across genres placing black as the blank colour, it was decided that where the limits of the space was reached, black should be used where these limitations were reached. The use of black was initially only required at either end of the space, with buildings running traverse along the long lengths of the space. This was to indicate the limits of the scene to the audience, but also to mask the walls and technical operations. However, when the move into the reflective zone was added, budgetary and spatial limitations prevented the use of the deli to travel through in order to reach the zone, and also prevented the building of a road continuation set in the area opposite the rubble where participants were eventually led through a door into the zone. Whilst a cloth or flats could have been constructed with this scene painted upon them, this would likely not be an accurate depiction due to the shallow, almost two-dimensional nature, and would cause a direct crash between reality and theatre when audiences would then be led through a cloth/flat of a road. The decision was therefore made that this section of the wall opposite the rubble would also be black, to extend the blank canvas onto which an audience could imagine the continuation of the scene. The use of heavy smoke and haze, along with dim lighting, meant that all black surfaces were less obvious to audiences, showing as darkness rather than surfaces until the latter stages of the scene, where smoke had lifted and projections drew attention to them.

Whether or not actors are used (the case for and against is made later), the Micro-Scene is concerned with how theatrical technologies and production techniques can provide an engaging experience. The question was asked of 9/11: can a Micro-Scene be successful when the scenography is the 'star of the show'? The most immediately visible example of this theatrical technology for an audience member is probably going to be the set. Where other technologies, such as lighting, sound and visual media are mostly supportive to a production (that is, their adjudged success is usually inversely proportionate to their visibility, or at least the awareness of them amongst audiences), the vast majority of a set must be visible in order to justify its existence. In an immersive environment, the significance of the set, and of its high visibility, become even more apparent to a set designer. Where, in a conventional proscenium-arch show, the set has to be of a high enough quality for audiences viewing from one side only, in an immersive environment this quality must be replicated on all sides that an audience could possibly position themselves on. The ability to provide a facade that ends abruptly behind a tormentor or masking flat is severely limited by a three-dimensional environment.

Conventional set construction techniques were reviewed, with timber framed hard and soft flats used in 9/11, as well as structures made of timber and metal (including rostra). Referring back to Alan Lane's description of his intentions with immersive theatre: to wrap an environment around an audience (cited earlier); it became important early in the planning phase to consider what was underneath the audience as well as in front and around them. The idea of the floorcloth - used in many musicals and opera productions - was considered as an obvious choice, though texture was added to the conventional visual-only examples of end-on theatre. Using the ideas of floorcloths and floor coverings taken from shows I have worked on in the past, it was concluded that a pale, dusty material was needed to cover all floor space, rubble, signs and buildings. In researching the material for this, certain restrictions were in place: the substance must closely resemble the pulverised concrete dust that engulfed lower Manhattan on September 11th; it must be safe to work in - with inhalation risk kept to a minimum, and no toxicity either through inhalation or in contact with the skin; it must be inexpensive enough to cover the whole space and still remain within budget (around £70 for floor); it must be readily available. Several materials were considered and experimented with: ash from burning paper was attempted, but could not be produced in quantities large enough for the operation (however small amounts were used to provide a distinctive smell and visible smouldering prior to each performance); ground cork was tried, but whilst it was utterly safe and also easy to distribute and clear, both colour and texture underfoot were not accurate enough. The final experiment was with fuller's earth - which provided accurate crumbly texture and colour, was safe to work with and was readily available. The one drawback was cost, with bulk packages of the substance not being easy to find as labelled. With research, came the knowledge that some cat litters are made from pure fuller's earth, and are available in large bags at very low cost. Forty bags of fuller's earth cat litter were distributed around the space, and ground into dust in places using bricks and manpower. Beige floorcloths were laid before this distribution, both to protect the theatre's black floor and to provide a similar colour underneath the 'dust' should any patches be kicked clear. A key element to this floor was the feel and sound of walking on it, not just the visual impact. The dust covering was made deep enough to provide the softer give underfoot, with real glass scattered throughout the space to give audible crunch to participants' steps (figure 8). As a finishing touch, along with the smouldering ash, hundreds of sheets of paper (with budgets, policies and other business-related information printed on them) were scattered throughout, and talcum powder was distributed to provide the taste and visual impairment of having a dust suspended in the air. The safety of this talc was checked with the manufacturer, in order to ensure the safety of both audiences and production staff. The talc um powder was added after attempts to cover actors in the cat litter failed. The granules were simply to large to stick to their clothes and hair, and so the talcum offered the immediate impact to audiences of seeing and knowing where these characters had been - as per famous images from the day.

If the street scene was to be the experiment of placing participants into a version of Devine's 'other world', then the front of house zone and reflective zone were to be bridges between the real world and the 'other world'. The front of house zone did not remove participants from the real world, but instead contextualised and prepared them for what they were about to experience. The reflective zone was to link the 'other world' of the street scene back to reality, offering a chance to reflect on the experience as an historical event relevant to their real world, rather than the present time that the theatricality was attempting to create. Research therefore looked to museum theatre for ideas of bridging the past and present, and for prompting reflection. The International Museum Theatre Alliance is an organisation that promotes the use of theatre within museum exhibits. Esther Tolkoff cites several examples of members of this organisation using performance to educate in this setting, including: the Science Museum of Minnesota portraying Charles Darwin and his wife discussing the ethics of prolonging life through medicine; the Lower East Side Tenement Museum in New York using actors to cast audience members as newly-arrived immigrants, who together explore the issues of such immigrants; and a new couple of different nationalities exploring the multi-cultural differences in Quebec, at the Musee Canadien des Civilisations (cited in Tolkoff, 1995, sections 5-6: 'Types of Plays' - 'Living History'). In initial performances of 9/11, the idea of incorporating theatre into a reflective area was taken from the examples seen in museums, and the reflective zone was set out as a makeshift evacuation shelter. It was dressed like a school hall, with temporary beds, discarded clothing and personal effects strewn around. However, the intention was to bridge participants from the 'other world' back into the real world, giving them the opportunity to reflect on how that past experience had affected them in the present, and so the set dressings strewn around did not suggest a return to the real world. There was simply too much stimulation in what was intended to be a calm, introspective space: participants in these early performances reported expecting more action to take place, and so it was necessary to remove any notion of theatricality, and instead look towards how museums provide invitation to visitors to learn about and reflect on an external event at their own pace. With a desire to be more akin to a museum space than a theatrical set, the reflective zone required little in the way of scenographic elements. Simple display boards and walls, were used to house images and stories from those who had been there. This information was presented in a plain, matter-of-fact way - no attempt was made to sensationalise or theatricalise. Lighting was kept to a dim, open white flood light, and the space was silent. As participants entered the space, a door into the front of house foyer was opened, indicating freedom to leave the experience whenever one wished.

Lighting

The Micro-Scene environment of 9/11, in which participants have the illusion of free will to move around and look at the set from multiple angles, must allow for infinite viewing points;

coming from a similar approach to theatre in the round, where almost every angle needs covering when designing lighting. The major difference here must be that instead of all audience members on the outside looking in, some will also be on the inside looking out, and on the inside looking further in, and every other possible permutation. The key is that,

"The immersive perspective enables the viewer to see from within the image." (Bay-Cheng et al, 2011: 47).

Whilst Bay-Cheng is not talking literally here, her observation on the participants' view and engagement with a piece must stretch to them actually being able to see what is going on from within the creation. Ignoring the staging format momentarily, Francis Reid discusses the formation of lighting design decisions, suggesting that the vast majority of plays have some grounding in reality, though accepts that divergence from such reality varies by degree from production to production. Reid therefore claims that all lighting designs should begin at reality, with particular attention paid to the extent of natural and naturally-found lighting sources in the real location to be represented:

"Total naturalism - or, at least, as close as we can get to it on the stage - is the style with the clearest logic and therefore the easiest to understand, if not always the easiest to achieve ." (Reid, 2002: 113)

Though Reid makes a valid point in terms of always starting with reality, the style of lighting design is an artistic choice that goes hand in hand with the concept of the director, and it must be emphasised that the degree of variation from reality can be as much as maintaining only a passing symbolism of reality at points. Whatever the artistic style, the overriding objective of any lighting design is "sufficient illumination to achieve positive visibility" (ibid.: 3). This is a roundabout way of stating that actors and scenery must be lit. The way I explain this theory to my students, is to say that the lighting designer has two objectives: 55% of his job is to make sure the audience can see what they need to see, and; 45% of his job is to symbolise other information, such as mood, time, pace etc. Of course, an artistic process cannot actually be easily dismissed in mathematical terms, however I find that highlighting Reid's idea, that you cannot begin to design art through light until you have fulfilled its basic technical function, gives a useful starting point to any design. This technical function, the need to illuminate for the audience's benefit, becomes much more challenging when placing an audience within the image - within the action. With no closer reference point than theatre in the round from which to begin, the two leading theories in lighting this format must be outlined: Reid proclaims that his preference is four lanterns at 90 degree intervals for each acting area; while Jackie Staines, who became a major exponent of lighting in the round whilst at the Stephen Joseph theatre - widely acknowledged as being the first In-The-Round theatre in the UK. Staines prefers to use three lanterns at 120 degree intervals per acting area (Staines, 2000: throughout - pp.19, 112, 122 as examples). For the 'other world' of the 9/11 street, it was intended to provide an illusion of being in the area at the time of the attacks. Staying close to naturalistic lighting was therefore desired, with the aim of trying to encourage immersion, and therefore engagement. The naturalistic presentation method was first defined by Stanley McCandless in 1932, and relies on two subtly different colours per area; one with a warm tint, and one with a cool, with each colour entering the acting area from a 45 degree angle. This 45 degree, two-tint method has been used as a basis for naturalistic lighting since. Lighting designers traditionally use profiles for long throws, applying a soft focus to retain the wash quality, whilst allowing them to blend with Fresnels used on the shorter throw distances. Here is a convention for producing naturalism that has stood the test of time. It is important to digress slightly here to emphasise that Reid suggests reality as a starting point for lighting design. I use the term naturalism here because no matter how close to reality a lighting design sits, it is still not going to offer 'real' lighting sources for the scene being played out (the exception being scenes that take place in a theatre, under theatrical lighting).

In keeping with Staines' method for lighting in the round, as well as Reid's method for starting with reality for all lighting designs, a three-point naturalistic wash was devised for 9/11 that were coloured with a combination of Lee 103 Straw, Lee 117 Steel Blue, and open white, in a series of one-kilowatt Fresnels arranged as per the lighting plan (Appendix F). Although these Fresnels were creating the illusion of natural daylight, it was a daylight that was mostly obscured by the dust of the nearby collapsed tower, and so they were used only at 25% intensity. It was also important to position them such that they did not provide illumination inside the deli, or cast light through windows from inside either building. Moving lights were used simply for ease of focusing and plotting, and provided a further point to several naturalistic wash areas, with straw filters applied to their outputs.

To return to the point on what to do with a lighting design once Reid's 'real' starting point has been established; the theatricalisation of a piece, or the removal from reality, often bears the best results when signalled by lighting. In stylised moments, hard-edged spotlights are often used with un-natural saturated colours washing an acting area. Musical theatre, being known for portraying clear removal from reality, often uses snaps between naturalistic and stylised - between subtle two-tint wash and saturated colour and hard edges - to clarify to the audience that they are removed from reality for the duration of the cue. The desire for naturalism presented a problem: even the most willing participant, who happily embraces the notion of suspending disbelief, will not forget they are in a theatre, and that it is not really the time or place that the scene is trying to create an illusion of. Thomas Scheff suggests that,

"At aesthetic distance the members of the audience become emotionally involved in the Drama, but not to the point where they forget that they are observers." (1979, cited in Grainger, 2010: 17).

He goes on to define "aesthetic distance" as being the simultaneous and equality of being both observer and participant. In the immersive

Micro-Scene of 9/11, audiences were observing their surroundings, but their presence within the set and their interactions with characters placed them also into the participant category. It can therefore be argued that Micro-Scene participants are good examples of Scheff's audience members, who cannot forget they are observing theatre.

Scheff's theory that audiences will never forget they are observers, on some level, 'permits' the shift into the unnatural for the firefighters' story. However, this shift does not sit well with the intention to place participants into Devine's 'other world'. For the unnatural shift into the firefighters' story, moving lights were able to cross fade to a dim Lee 181 Congo Blue - a very deep purple - that, in tandem with the blackout of all naturalistic lighting, was the primary indicator to the audience that they were being removed from the street. I will discuss the reasons behind this removal from naturalism later, though at this point acknowledge that the method could never work with both acknowledgement of Scheff's claim and of the desire to create illusion of the 'other world'.

Within the street scene, the other use of lighting was as a practical traffic signal. Being RGB (Red Green Blue) LED fixtures, the Red and Green signals were accurately coloured, whereas the amber was either too yellow or too green. To rectify this, several sheets of Lee 103 filter were applied in front of the LEDs, which mostly resolved the problem. The other problem with the LEDs was that each LED capsule was approximately one inch in diameter, with the whole light output provided by 36 of these large LEDs. In a practical piece of scenery, in an intimate environment, these larger LEDs did not give the same uniform colour face as one would expect to find on a traffic signal. In later stages of the experiment, thick frost was applied to the front of the LED fixtures, and although this helped it did not entirely eliminate the problem. Whilst other fixtures, or indeed a fixture designed specifically to signal traffic, would provide LEDs more tightly packed, the project was limited to the Chroma-Q Colour Punches loaned to it free of charge by a lighting supplies company.

The reflective zone used only two single cell floods to illuminate the space. As this zone was intended not to actively engage participants onto a particular area or event, it was important that the lighting illuminated the whole space evenly. With the emphasis on the audience to form their own emotional response here, it was important not to use any colour or tight angles to suggest desired response to participants: they must know they are free to form their own responses without pressure from the author or other participants. The floods were therefore kept open white, with no highlighting of particular sections.

Once the performance had begun, the cueing and operation was simple. The show from the lighting board operator's point of view was split into two cues, with smoke, haze and a running traffic light sequence effect layered via manual sub-masters. A Jands Vista T4 console was utilised to run the show; partly due to the ease of patching, plotting and moving light operation; and partly due to this desk being one of three in stock, and therefore would not drain the limited budget. Though the cue list went through several permutations to match the state of the performance at various stages, the final performance consisted of two cues: the naturalistic preset, using the straw, steel and open white Fresnels and straw-coloured moving wash fixtures, which remained throughout the female university students' dialogue; and the highly stylised firefighters' story audio and projection state, which used the Congo blue moving wash fixtures, and a harsh white, hard-edged spot on a fireman's radio on the rubble (figure 9). The choice behind using the Congo blue and harsh spot was reached through deciding to make it very clear to audiences that they were exiting the street scene, and could in fact be anywhere around the site of the attacks, or even in the house of the widow of a firefighter killed in the action. Whilst the radio placed on the rubble was part of reality - it was a piece of the scene itself - the harsh spot was necessary to place the audience at arm's reach of the reality of it.

Sound

"Sound Design is not a dramatic or a performance art. It is quintessentially a theatre art... [it] cannot exist without its acoustic environment; without its attendant theatre." (Brown, 2010: 5)

To summarise Ross Brown's introductory observations on sound; we are - in the 21st Century developed world, at least - immersed in audio (ibid.: 1-3). The real world has us enveloped in noises and music, and overspill from the noise and music of others. Brown observes that this immersion is not helpful to sound designers (ibid.: 3), and suggests that a critical perspective is necessary to unpick and reconstruct an environment on stage.

The above direct quote, taken from the same introductory chapter, highlights an important point: sound is a scenographic element, to be balanced within the mise-en-scène. Whilst there are examples that can argue the case for sound alone being able to dramatically perform - many music albums are said by their creators to tell a story; and radio plays, though relying on dialogue, are still using nothing but sound to perform (Brown acknowledges this counter-argument without giving examples) - 9/11 is concerned with the creation of a multi-sensory experience, and so it is the mise-en-scène as a total environment that is to be considered here.

In producing soundscapes and effects for a show, the starting point can be reality. Brown comments on the three sonic worlds that the advent of electronic sound reproduction in theatre gave us:

"the 'real' world of actor's [sic] voices, stage movements and the audience's coughs, the world of the 'live' noises-off - the thunder sheet, the 'practical' telephone or doorbell and the coconut shell, which the audience accepted by convention but which were obviously live but not 'real', and a separate, mediatised electroacoustic world of replayed sound, which was 'realistic' but not 'real' or live." (ibid.: 31)

Some consideration of these three sonic worlds was present in the planning process for 9/11. The 'real' sonic world included the actors' voices and the crunching of glass and rubble underfoot. This crunching could fall either into the 'real' category or the 'live': whilst it is a real sound of glass breaking, made even more real by the fact that it was a direct result of a participant's movement, it could be argued that the glass is not a real result of a plane hitting a nearby building. How far does one take the definition of realism in this context? The crunching underfoot could therefore be a 'real' world sound, or it could simply be a 'live' sound that offers representation of a location. The third world - the mediated electroacoustic world - is easier to identify within 9/11. Participants entered into a soundscape - a naturalistic background track that offered information keys tied into location.

John Leonard discusses his methods for creating a variety of soundscapes, giving A Streetcar Named Desire as an example (Leonard, 2002: 146). For this production, he produces a soundscape that includes the sound of a jazz saxophone down the street, clatter of the elevated railroad, a distant train whistle, the sound of a shower in the next room and thunder in middle distance, with music coming from an onstage radio. Leonard's soundscapes can be broadly split into the following sections: a drone - using low-key elements of railroad noises to bed the track, giving the opportunity to loop, whilst also giving generic location hints; secondary events - the distant saxophone and thunder - give clues to location, time, culture and weather; and primary events - the radio and the shower - setting the scene for an audience. For 9/11, the drone included distant chatter and regular foot and road traffic. Sirens can form a part of the drone, a secondary event or a primary event, due to it being an expected feature of a New York street scene on any normal day. In 9/11, the difference between a siren being a drone, a secondary event, or a primary event, was made by differences in speaker routing and volume. Much quieter sirens that were spread across a wide degree of direction gives the impression of distance, and is, by itself, not unusual for an urban environment. Louder and more directed sirens, passing quickly from one location to another, give the impression of closer emergency. Again, nearby sirens are not unusual for an urban environment, and so the layering of many sirens, across all directions and implied distances were offered as a secondary event in the soundscape. Regular, crunching bodies were routed to a speaker behind the vanishing 'road' projection, as a subtle bed. This audio was based on the true stories of many people who jumped from the burning towers, dying instantly and loudly upon impact with the glass canopy or concrete below. The low-volume, repetitive nature of this element was intended to form part of the drone; in order to highlight through its inconspicuousness how normal this extraordinary event had become at this scene. One louder instance of a crunching body, used after several minutes of silence, was used as a primary event at the end of the young man on phone section, to represent his girlfriend jumping from the tower.

The soundscape was intended to immediately place participants into the 'other world' - by including walkie-talkie noise, sirens, chatter and both vehicle and pedestrian movement. However, whilst I wanted audiences to immediately know where they are, the desire to create the illusion of a street scene (in order to suspend disbelief and further engagement into the environment), meant that the initial soundscape must also be subtle. The resulting track can be heard in Video Appendix D (between 00:00 and 02:57), and this track was sent to the outputs behind the drapes and office building at differing volumes (though all very low) to allow audiences to be surrounded by the sound. Upon one of the female student characters pressing play on her camcorder, the sound cue to play the 'dorm girls' audio was executed. The idea was to synchronise the playing of the video on the tiny screen; to retain the naturalistic style, although by using the PA system to provide extra volume for all participants to hear. Experiments were carried out with the audio also coming from the camcorder, along with the video, but whilst the small screen added to the tension and feeling of 'being there' - the audio was not powerful enough to reach a fuller audience, without losing their engagement altogether, and so use of Brown's 'mediated electroacousticity' was employed in order to ensure audibility. The final cue list for the sound operator can be found in Appendix H.

Audio was necessary to engage audiences into a three-dimensional world, and to promote this idea, speakers were placed at various points within two of the three spaces (see Appendix G). The front of house space required audio from the news programming of the morning of the attacks, and the best way to do this was to ensure that the audio was attached to the video file, and streamed to the front of house television screens with the volume set on the screens themselves. As the video was edited to flow more smoothly within the timeframe required (around 15 minutes of mundane video before the scheduled show time, plus 2 minutes of attack footage after the scheduled start time), the audio was detached from the video, edited and reattached at the final stage. This ensured that appropriate audio continued on over the text information that ran at the end of both front of house videos. The Final Cut package by Apple was utilised for the video and audio editing in the front of house zone. The audio in the street scene required more involvement: speakers were placed around the space. Spot effect speakers were placed underneath the rubble, for an initial walkie-talkie effect (the fireman's radio being placed on top of the rubble). Other speakers were placed behind the office building, the drapes near the main entrance, the cyclorama and the drapes on the rubble side of the theatre. Speakers were connected to various different outputs to allow for independent control - different audio tracks being played through different locations. Audio tracks were created using audio captured on September 11th, and by mixing in theatrical cheating when necessary to aid understanding of the environment. For example, the end of the firefighters' story triggered an effect that included processed creaking door audio to suggest the distant strains of a building about to collapse. Audacity and Adobe Audition were both used to edit the audio for the street scene, and a laptop running Show Control Software (SCS) through a multi-channel external sound card provided the PA system. A further sound source was placed in the deli, by way of setting up the television set showing 'live' news coverage of the events and playing audio through the internal speakers. Using a DVD player for the audio and video source, and the speakers within the television set, this source was not required to be linked to SCS.

The firefighters' audio, however, was a heavily edited montage of conversations extracted from the Fire Department's radio transmissions from the day, intended to clearly remove participants from the representation of reality offered in the street scene up until this point. The intention was to create a busy, multi-layered walkie-talkie soundscape that immersed participants into an aural environment. Along with the lighting transition into Congo blue and a harsh spotlight on the radio, the soundscape was a clear stylistic presentation. This was achieved through the layering of many transmissions from responders on the ground, some of which were edited into gaps - so that when the whole soundscape was heard, the story of the firefighters in general was told, rather than of one person. It was intended that audiences could listen to the 'behind the scenes' dialogue and gain a different insight into the traumas suffered by many individuals on the day. In editing and summarising an entire group of people's experiences and journeys into one story package, suspension of disbelief would not be possible had I presented this in a naturalistic way. It was therefore necessary to make it very obvious that naturalism was not the intention at this stage. I will discuss the reasons for this change in style in more detail below.

Visual Media

Visual media were employed for a number of reasons: as 'moving scenery' in the street scene (with the deli television); to contextualise for audiences arriving and remaining in the venue and in the street scene (front of house videos and deli television); and to provide further static scenery beyond the confines of the physical space 9/11 was limited to (the cyclorama projection).

With the projection of the destruction in the street on the cyclorama behind the rubble; care was taken to follow the advice of Julia Bardsley, director of The Divine Trilogy (2009):

"I didn't want the tyranny of the white projection screen at the back of the space [...] I also didn't want the information in the video to be simply a light source – even though that can be interesting as well." (cited in Johnson, 2010: 17)

Bardsley goes on to discuss how she used gauze to project on to, and through, in order to integrate the projections with the live action. This demonstrates an awareness on Bardsley's part that video projection is in danger of separating itself from the rest of the scene, and therefore splitting the audience's attention between the fragments. Scenographer Pamela Howard states that,

"The mise-en-scène is validated when the direction, the use of space and light, and the scenography all speak with one voice." (2009: 135)

Frank Ludwig agrees, believing that,

"The story is often not primary; the story is in balance with the visual imagery, the sound, and the interactivity." (2011: 57)

It is the balance that is deemed most important by Howard and Ludwig, and Bardsley agrees by consciously avoiding the overpowering of one particular element - in her case the projection screen. The use of black in the projections, and in the screen medium, allows the video and remaining mise-en-scène to be less disjointed.

For the image of continuing road and rubble, I did deliberate at length about the medium on which to project, as well as whether the image was necessary at all. At an early stage in production, I tried projecting through gauze for this element, as Bardsley did in The Divine Trilogy, but whilst the projection screen was better integrated into the set, the result was a wholly unrealistic double image on both the gauze and the wall opposite, whilst also showing the projector and other mechanics in the backstage area behind. By leaving out the image altogether, the remaining options would have been to build a vanishing road set or to place a plain black surface. The road set was not possible due to the lack of space, and the experiment with extending the black surface to behind the rubble resulted in disjointing the set - presenting too much blank space. The final experiment, and the method that was retained throughout public performance, was to use the cyclorama that Bardsley tried to avoid. In order to integrate this scenic element, care was taken to ensure that every visible inch of the cloth was covered in the image (borders would immediately scream 'picture frame' in the same way a proscenium arch would have done). To successfully cover the entire surface in the image, a projector with a very wide lens (38 degree beam width) was employed, throwing an an image over an average distance of five metres. The image itself was adjusted using Adobe Lightroom, so that an overall hazy straw tint covered the frame, blending in well with the lighting state. Thick smoke and haze was used around the rubble-end of the space to further blend in the image, meaning it was visible behind the rubble, but took effort and care to see through the smoke and establish minor detail.

There still remains the issue of projection jarring against the surrounding environment, when aiming to create the illusion of the 'other world'. Projection is fundamentally unrealistic, unless used to create a video-centric scenic item, such as a video advertising screen within a street scene. Video projection has been increasingly used over the last decade in place of physical scenery, sometimes out of artistic design, but often out of cost considerations. Whilst it has found its place as a 'mood enhancer' in stylised theatre and rock musicals, it is perhaps not always enhancing the mise-en-scène, but overshadowing the sum total. For example, David Barbour suggests that the 2006 Johnny Cash show Ring of Fire was so short-lived, was due in some part to the intrusiveness of the technology in an attempt to create a "homespun atmosphere" (Barbour, 2011: 31). Animated projections also bear the scars of failed productions, including a Guys and Dolls revival in 2009 (where Barbour quotes David Rooney;

"The fussy video input constantly pulls focus, overwhelming the actors and snuffing out both the human drama and the comedy," 2011: 31)

Also refer to Lloyd Webber's brief Broadway failure, The Woman In White, which attempted to use an,

"...enormous curved [projection] screen, featuring animated imagery that completely dwarfed both the actors and story." (Barbour, 2011: 31)

Whilst retaining an unnatural style, the scale of the projection can also have a detrimental effect on an appropriately styled performance. Where projections cannot be diegetically integrated within a Micro-Scene, it should be noted that an attempt to pass them off extra-diegetically is likely to fragment audience's attention, thus removing levels of immersion and engagement between participants and environment. Putting it simply; creators of 'realistic' scenes should be aware that if they are to use video projection, by failing to integrate it realistically into their scene, they are in danger of losing their audience. It is clear that to avoid fulfilling Barbour's fears on an unbelievable or over-scaled projection overshadowing a show, such media must be well integrated within it. Bardsley's methods with gauze and black image is one method of more seamless integration, and the other is to use visual media only diegetically. Indeed, Wendall Harrington's claim that audience imagination is more powerful than imposed imagery (cited earlier) can extend to physical scenery also. It is an underlying theory behind the use of black in a set where accuracy cannot be recreated.

The television in the deli was used to play 'live' news coverage of the events happening in the vicinity. The media was originally sourced from recordings of NBC morning news on the day, found on YouTube; the stream captured and downloaded, before being converted to a format that could be read by a standard DVD player. This enabled the deli television to be a standalone audio and video source; not relying on the media servers that fed the front of house screens, and not requiring the main PA system for audio. The intention of this video was twofold: to provide context and ongoing background information; and to provide richer scenery from another direction - thus improving the level of 'reality' and therefore another tool to engage audiences.

The front of house videos were the largest visual media elements used, although perhaps not the most prominent. The first screen was intended to begin to run approximately sixteen minutes before the scheduled performance time. It ran with mundane, breakfast magazine programming up until the scheduled performance time, before the news breaks, live on air, that a plane has crashed into the World Trade Centre. The intention was not to draw attention to the screen, which was permanently fixed to the wall and so became part of the furniture of the foyer seating area. The programming would offer context to participants who had limited or no knowledge of the events, and would remind older audiences that initially, news reporters and the public in general thought the first plane hitting was accidental. The awareness that whilst almost all adult participants would have seen the images broadcast from New York many times, they are unlikely to have seen the news break, live - but will probably have tuned in during the unfolding of the events. The 'live' breaking story therefore offers participants a chance to experience the huge contrast between the very ordinary interview with an author, and the upbeat weather forecast, and the tragedy that followed. Approximately two minutes after the scheduled performance time (to ensure all participants have seen this contextualising video; latecomers were not admitted), the 'live' news feed dissolved into simple black screens with white text, giving the basic facts about the impacts of the two planes. This text sequence was intended to set the scene, and also give instruction on where to move next, without a shepherding usher wrenching participants from their thoughts. An arrow simply pointed towards a corridor, where a second screen then came into life. This clip was from the same news channel, but showed the first tower collapsing, live on air. The audience were now aware of the point in time at which they enter the street: after the first tower had collapsed. They are then able to place causes behind every element of destruction they see, as well as the reasoning behind the characters they will meet. Some participants noted that the news anchors still aren't sure what is happening at this point: the male anchor during the second clip suggests a "chunk of the building has fallen off the side," with confusion at this stage over how much has actually collapsed. This ambiguity would later manifest itself in the uncertainty of two of the characters within the street scene.

Along with physical scenery, use of the three principle theatrical technologies - lighting, sound and projection - can create a complete location. It is the design and use that will determine whether each has been successfully crafted in order to maximise engagement from the audience. The intention with these scenographic elements is to provide a location that can transport an audience member to another world and time without the need for actors. If a Micro-Scene can fulfil this aim, then any use of actors within the scene will only serve, and indeed must only be used, to enhance realism.

Actors and Props

Props were kept to a minimum. Each of the three characters were based on accounts, videos and photographs of real people, and so only those items that the real people held or needed were transformed into props in 9/11. The two female university students (the 'NYU Dorm Girls') had run out of their high-rise dormitory building without getting dressed. They wore pyjamas, and had been woken by the first impact and proceeded to film it, and so had only a video camera in their hand when the second plane hit and they fled in a panic. Their only prop was this camcorder, that had to be capable of showing what they had filmed earlier that morning. A real camcorder was used, and the video by the real university students (acquired from the History Channel), that inspired the two characters, was pre-loaded onto its memory card. The young man whose girlfriend fell out of a high window in a building on fire needed only his costume to suggest his purpose before the event (jeans and a hooded top, and a satchel, to suggest he was on his way to university). The method of his story delivery was through our observing of his phone conversation with his girlfriend, as he stood in the street trying to see her. His only prop was therefore his mobile phone, which needed to be able to withstand the shocked character dropping the phone.

The decision to include actors was taken after careful consideration of the primary research question. In focusing on the use of theatrical technologies to create an immersive environment, there is the possibility that actors are omitted altogether in the interests of ensuring that only theatrical technologies are used to immerse audiences into the 'other world'. Coney Theatre Company's A Small Town Anywhere at the Battersea Arts Centre in 2009 used no actors, but instead cast audience members as community figures in a small town set built within the theatre. Participants were then left to get on with creating and shaping the narrative, having received some information on what it was generally about beforehand. The interactivity existed between each participant, and between participants and the set and props within. However, A Small Town Anywhere was not only a piece of fiction, but also presented as a game (Coney, 2012, section 5: 'Comment on devising process'). A sense of playfulness is expected of the audience here, which does in turn allow for the unrealism of pretending you know your fellow participants when in truth they are mostly strangers. This type of interactive theatre is by default immersive - each participant immerses themselves into a role, and in turn immerse that role into a 'town' where interaction with props and other role-playing participants is the main point of the exercise. However, A Small Town Anywhere also holds much commonality with the traditional murder mystery weekend: Coney's style of actor-less interactivity works because it is a game. To create a narrative, though, they still relied on human participants. If the subject of the narrative was more serious, or perhaps non-fictional, then the murder mystery style of casting audiences as the only characters in the show would not work - the playfulness would not be appropriate. Using an historical event, like the September 11th attacks, requires a higher level of accuracy in order to avoid the performance becoming distasteful. It must be presented in a style that sits well with an intended accuracy: for a subject so evocative, audiences may be offended at a playful approach. Tastefulness can be better achieved through gentle immersion of the audience through the chance to explore in their own time, to observe from a safe distance, and to interact with the environment as they feel comfortable. It is assumed that participants - at least the adults - will have experienced a negative emotional response to the attacks: shock, sadness, fear, panic. By including other participants in the scene, in the city, with them will help create a safe environment in which to guide audiences through their own emotional responses. Audiences will have each other to judge what is an acceptable or expected response to the scene they are immersed in, but the responses of the 'locals' is of greater significance to them. These local characters could be implied, or they could be present.

Alke Gröppel-Wegener points out two problems with faithful re-creations of historical events. She states that it would be,

"Fairly expensive to populate an environment with actors who are knowledgeable enough about a subject." (Gröppel-Wegener, 2011: 43)

Indeed, expense was a factor in 9/11, but more of a consideration was the requirement by the host school management that the project offers a learning experience for students. In this scenario, whilst the actors came free of charge, the cost was wrapped up in their quality: although they were talented, helpful, and willing, they were after all, children with limited acting experience. In order to minimise losses in this sense, it is necessary to minimise the use of low-quality actors. Gröppel-Wegener also cites an argument that questions whether or not actors - and indeed any attempt at faithful re-creation - are needed at all.

"[Some aspects of history] can only be enacted to a limited extent. We can't kill people on the battlefields; we can't have dysentery and disease in medieval re-

enactments. Do we debase people's understanding of the past because such events can't be fully reproduced?" (Rumble, 1989 cited in Gröppel-Wegener, 2011: 43)

In pointing to Rumble's argument, Gröppel-Wegener makes an interesting point, applicable to the 9/11 project: if faithful re-creations will never be possible with some historical events (I include the September 11th attacks here), then why bother trying to? After all, audiences are still capable of learning and engaging with the subject without full, realistic re-creation. She makes her thoughts clearer and more specific to the use of actors, when suggesting that,

"An immersive experience can also be arrived at through non-manned strategies." (Gröppel-Wegener, 2011: 43).

However, in removing all actors, 9/11 would perhaps resemble a static snapshot of an event or location, rather than a progressive narrative. In relying on the 'live' television coverage playing in the deli, or other visual media, to give a progressive narrative, the Micro-Scene can simply become a video art exhibition with an over-elaborate viewing room.   Imperial War Museum North, Salford, is one example of where theatrical technologies alone are used to drive a story. The Big Picture Show is a multi-media presentation, utilising several projectors and a surround-sound PA system to immerse visitors into the sounds and images of war. There is lots going on, with different images and strands of the narrative being played simultaneously in different areas of the walls and floor, but the same narrative could have been delivered (and emotional responses triggered) through a conventional cinema or television screen: the environment and method of presentation adds very little to the experience, as it is the power of the stories told, sounds played and images shown that engages those audiences who choose to stay and watch.

Consideration was given to the world that 9/11 is representing - a street near the World Trade Centre. This world would be expected to contain people: people at the original scene were watching in awe, stood in shock, running or crying over missing loved ones, chatting to each other, or simply wishing to be with other people in a time of great danger. In order to allow greater engagement and empathy with the experiences and emotions of other human beings, the practice of using actors to move a narrative along can potentially deepen the level at which a participant is immersed into Devine's 'other world': if the location in which one places the audience is one that would naturally include other people, then it may be beneficial in prompting greater suspension of disbelief to offer some of what the audience would expect to find, thus offering a deeper level of immersion. Kevin Moore discusses the power of the 'Triple Real'.

"Triple real...real things in their real place as experienced by a real person." (Moore, 1997: 142)

Here, Moore is suggesting that the use of 'real' people in museum theatre is a key component of a successful experience (interestingly, Gröppler-Wegener acknowledges the problematisation of the term 'reality' in this context, 2011: 41). By using live characters within the 9/11 street scene, audiences are offered the widest range of interactive potential. More significantly for the creation of the Micro-Scene, it is the interaction - even on a minimal, environment-only level - that provides a greater immersion into the illusion of the environment being created. The shows of Punchdrunk and Slung Low have arguably triggered a powerful sense of personal immersion into their performances through using actors: either to guide participants through the narrative; or to further remove or reduce the sense of disbelief amongst audiences, through providing people naturally expected in a location to reinforce the illusion.

It is this quest for representing the street as an illusion of reality that also provided a severe limitation on 9/11: in placing actors into the scene, they must be of high quality, appropriate age and appearance. Being limited to using only school students as actors (due to both budgetary requirements and the condition set by the venue that 9/11 must be a piece of coursework for students) meant that in order to maintain appropriate age, appearance and quality, the characters I could present were restricted to three students, who could get away with playing possibly three years older than themselves. These characters were the two female "dorm girls" and a lone male who spoke to his girlfriend on the phone as she died. The preparation of the actors took the form of several workshops, throughout the window of the two weeks they were available (though only in 45 minute blocks per day). Narratives were outlined, with 'milestone events' being decided upon for each of the two sections. The actors were then required to improvise their way from one milestone to the next. These improvisations were fleshed out through questioning them in role, and forum theatre taking place with other performing arts students. The two girls struggled for ideas on how to improvise the story of their journey from apartment to street, and so a script was written for them. As rehearsals progressed they began to go off script and add their own details, some of which had to be checked against fact for accuracy. Once each actor was comfortable and confident with the narrative that they had to drive, they were coached through possible interactions with participants. Instructions were given that they must share their world with anyone else in it - that if they see audience members, they must acknowledge them. The dorm girls were first into the scene, and were tasked with setting the convention. They were instructed to make it clear to participants that talking was allowed, questions should be asked, and that two-way interaction was expected as much as one would find in the real streets after such an event. In order to set this convention, telling audiences how they are expected to interact, their opening line was always a question; "Oh my God, are you all OK?" or, "Is anyone hurt?" Attached to the question was direct eye contact and further probing questions if participants did not immediately acknowledge them.

With the young man on the phone, it was difficult to allow him to include the audience once he started getting emotional, as it would not be realistic: a man in that situation would not be remotely aware of the other people around him. When workshopping, it was experimented with him first asking for a phone from members of audience, to interact with them, before taking one from another character (to ensure the safety of the phone). However this proved to disrupt the flow from a theatrical point of view. In the latter stages of 9/11, his interaction with the audience was limited to moving through the crowd of participants, looking for a better view of the tower, muttering "excuse me" as he pushed past.

There was also a desire to use more actors in the scene and have their own stories continuing on all at once, to allow audience members to choose different people to watch or engage with, rather than focusing everyone onto one point at a time. This experiment was not possible at this time due to the lack of good quality actors. Evaluating the success of this approach takes place in the concluding sections of this book.

Delivering the three angles of personal impact (terrified bystanders, grief-stricken loved one, brave rescue workers) that drove the narrative and provoked the all-important personal response would not be possible without resorting to unnatural projections or voice overs for the entirety of the piece. The alternative would be to persuade audiences to take on roles themselves in order to explore the emotional impacts of these three angles, but this brings us into 'Murder Mystery' territory, much like Coney Theatre's A Small Town Anywhere, and the associated playfulness of such tactics. And so a key factor that swung the decision in favour of using actors was, perhaps surprisingly, the desire to rely on technology to explore personal impacts and responses. The "dorm girls" were based on two real people who lived in an apartment overlooking the World Trade Centre towers. From early on in the planning phase, there was a desire to show the audience their relatively unknown video recording from that morning. The video starts with relatively calm interest in the 'accidental tragedy' of the period just after the first plane hit, and captures the second plane's impact, before going on to document the girls' panic and flight from their tall building. Their angle was inviting as a piece of theatre, because it offered a very personal angle on such a global event, but it was a response that was experienced by many thousands of others in the same position: the realisation that they were under attack and could not defend themselves. In order for this arresting footage to be shown to the audience, without breaking the illusion of the 'real' street scene, it was necessary to find a realistic method of presentation. The video camera prop mentioned above was the solution, as it offered the chance to reinforce the ending of the video, which shows the girls fleeing their apartment in a rush, camera still in hand. The intention was to create a real sense that the street scene housing the participants did have a 'before' and will have an after, again reinforcing the realism. Returning to the point that the desire to focus on technology swaying the decision in favour of using actors; it was a simple case of needing the owner of the video camera to hold and operate the video camera. This in turn required dialogue to support the video presentation: the actors supported the technology in this case.

Operating the show

Despite offering an illusion of free will in which participants could explore their surroundings, the entire experience had to be tightly stage managed to ensure the progress of the narrative and the coherence of various technological aspects of the story-telling.

The crew consisted of a lighting operator, sound operator, projectionist and visual media operator (the various television screens and media server). Another member of crew was utilised to stage manage the participants discretely, being dressed as a member of the audience, and sitting in the foyer with friends before the show. She was instructed to only act if necessary, by drawing attention to key visual elements of the narrative (getting up and standing in front of a screen, for example) or in extreme cases, suggesting the group go through a door. She is classed as crew, rather than performer, because her sole objective was the smooth running of the show, and not to provide any further engagement or narrative to participants. The whole crew and technology was directed by a Deputy Stage Manager, who offered stand-by and go cues to each operator via cue lights. As most of the crew did not have any sight of the performance spaces, the DSM was positioned behind the office building facade, with a spy hole cut through a poster to allow her to follow visual cues.

Significant shift in style within the street scene

With all the explanation and justification for how scenography and actors were used to create the illusion of being in a New York street on the morning of the attacks, it is important to explain and justify the reason for the departure from this illusion within the street scene for the firefighters' story.

This third narrative angle on the attacks was intended to provoke thought about the actions of the firefighters at the scene on the day, and needed to tell the story of the typical firefighter's experience.

Reality was stretched beyond acceptance in early experiments, as if audiences were kept in the 'world' of this street for the delivery of the firefighters' story, it would have perhaps been necessary to use actors to portray the characters and play out the narrative. The absence of the type, age and quality of actor required to play these parts would have detracted from the believability of the piece, reducing engagement in the environment. More importantly, however, is that the piece would have been heavily weighted in favour of the actor driving the narrative, and 9/11 would not be best exploring the notion of a Micro-Scene relying primarily on theatrical technologies.

Consideration also had to be given to the intention to provoke an emotional response through experiencing the Micro-Scene. The ultimate objective was to give participants enough stimuli to begin to form thought, opinion and empathy with all of those affected by September 11th - but more importantly, to enable them to capture their response and articulate it to each other, to the creators or on paper. The reflective zone became the key component in this sense, as without it, thoughts and emotions would possibly not have been consolidated into a coherent response. The departure from the world the street in the firefighters' story, apart from allowing the piece to focus on technology for a few minutes, allowed 9/11 to bridge the gap between the 'other world' that Devine discusses, and the real world. For these few minutes, participants were gently brought back to themselves, clearly told that they are now in a theatre space in a building that they arrived in earlier - that the illusion is over - and therefore preparing them for the museum-like (and therefore the real world of the) reflective zone. For this reason, the story was unreal: the soundscape played from all directions, cutting from left, to centre, to right, to far right in random order; the projected text was simple white on black, away from the 'real' street set and thrown onto the black boundary wall, highlighting the theatre structure (and thus the real world) itself. I will judge the success of this tactic in the concluding sections of this book.

Micro-Scene: immersion and/ or interactivity?

Looking once again at notable British immersive theatre companies; Punchdrunk, Slung Low, Badac and Blast Theory (http://www.blasttheory.co.uk) amongst others, there is a common theme that becomes evident throughout their repertoires. All of these companies have offered shows that attempt to invoke an emotional response in their audiences through extreme terror and fear. For example, Punchdrunk's It Felt Like A Kiss includes a character that chases audiences down a corridor whilst wielding a chainsaw. Badac's The Factory at the Edinburgh Festival in 2008 used actors screaming expletives and banging metal sheets at audience members in order to re-create the unpleasantness of Auschwitz concentration camp. Slung Low used similar methods in They Only Come At Night: Resurrections where innocent blood-type registering at the start of the show sows the seed for fear later on, enhanced by power surges, blackouts, and being locked in a confined space. The regularity of contemporary immersive shows that use extreme fear in an attempt to engage its audience has resulted in a number of theatre critics writing as though immersive theatre and attempts at instilling extreme fear are inseparable:

"[Actors] led me through into a disorientingly cold and inhospitable space, instead of feeling a frisson of "what now?" I just thought, "Oh, not blindfolded again"." (Higgins, 2009)

"This crass attempt to chill the blood brought mine close to the boil." (Hickling, 2009)

"[Immersive theatre] cannot make us fear for our lives; any production that stubbornly refuses to accept this is bound to fail." (Gardner, 2010)

However, there are examples of shows by these immersive theatre companies that sit at the other end of the spectrum. Punchdrunk's Sleep No More did not attempt to crassly scare audiences, or inflict extreme multi-sensory stimulation upon participants. Based on Macbeth, it invoked unease, and even fear, as participants were free to roam a vast set sprawled over six floors of a warehouse. But it is the very nature of the narrative and the locations that were enough to make audiences nervous, bringing them out of their comfort zones without any shouting, chasing or threats of violence (indeed, the whole experience is wordless). Punchdrunk have shown both sides of the immersive coin; that fear and terror is useful in prompting engagement, and that the subject and environment alone can bring a deeper and more instinctive response and engagement from participants. Other examples exist, but the line can become blurred between immersive and promenade theatre. Slung Low's Helium at the Barbican Theatre, London (2008) is one such show. Straddling the genres of immersive, promenade and intimate theatres, observers are guided through a series of installations, where they observe a section of narrative alone. They are told that characters will not be able to see them, and therefore no interaction can take place. In considering this influence in the definition of the Micro-Scene, the key point is that there is no interaction: whilst audiences are immersed into several superficial environments, they are not truly immersed into these actual locations - they could be watching this play on a pre-recorded DVD, and still receive exactly the same narrative: Helium is entirely one-way; audiences are recipients of the narrative, not participants. Another, rather over-simplified, way of looking at it is to think of the famous philosophical question, "if a tree falls in the forest with nobody around to hear it, does it make a sound?" In immersive theatre the question could be, "if a participant is immersed in an environment and no (actor) acknowledges him, is he really in that environment?" As with any art form, individual works cannot always be easily categorised, and it would serve primarily to distract focus if I were to discuss all examples of work that hold some commonality with what I am trying to achieve. 9/11 aims to present a more natural environment that, like Sleep No More, relies on the narrative and theatrical technologies to forge an emotional engagement and response. By using a real event, and real news footage of that event to set the scene, the Micro-Scene relies on memories and understanding of that real world event to evoke emotional response, rather than fear from the contrived theatrical experience alone.

In Sleep No More; characters do not speak throughout the piece, and audiences are instructed not to speak. Even so, the show is offers an example of immersive design that is inherently interactive. In this show, characters dance with participants, but in other immersive theatre pieces, interaction between the two parties can be anything from eye contact to full-on conversation. Intimate theatre - an extreme form of immersive and interactive theatre - even sees audience members lying naked in a bath while the performer bathes them, before lying in bed together spooning (cuddling), actor feeding the participant chocolate (Adrian Howells' The Pleasure Of Being: Washing, Feeding, Holding, 2011). What defines a piece of interactive theatre is, according to Gary Izzo, that,

"The participant co-creates the scene with the actor, but on the actor's terms, and within the general goals of the performance." (Izzo, 1997: 26)

This does not happen in 9/11: participants do co-create the scene with the actor, as the dialogue that takes place is able to be manipulated by participants; but the outcome is not general. Izzo defines participatory theatre as being,

"Where there is a fixed outcome to the story [...] arrived at through a finite number of scenes that must be presented in a certain order, one after the other... [and the] audience participant responds or reacts to the production but does not alter it." (ibid.: 22-23, his emphasis)

Izzo is suggesting that participatory theatre is a diluted version of interactive theatre, but it is a definition that describes 9/11. Participants were stage-managed through a mapped-out order of events, and shepherded towards a final outcome. No matter where their reactions and dialogue went, the actors and crew would always guide the experience onto the next milestone. It is worth noting that Izzo is pre-occupied with a participant's interaction with actors when defining the genre. Looking at audience interaction with the environment as a whole is more appropriate to the definition and formation of the Micro-Scene. This interaction can be simple - the feeling of walking on dust, ash and broken glass in 9/11, and the ability to touch, taste and smell the environment. Applying Izzo's definitions of interactive theatre, it can be argued that in 9/11 offering participants the chance to be introspective, and to write their personal reflections on the wall, each individual forms their own unique outcome; thus creating interactive theatre on an individual level, and not participatory theatre.

Thus the argument can be made that every immersive theatre production is inherently interactive - with the level of interaction on a sliding scale. But this can also be true of any performance. The director Peter Brook points out that,

"You don't have to 'join in' to participate fully in a performance. A successful interaction with the stage demands a reactive audience; that's how any good theatre happens, even in the West End." (cited in Coveney, 2010)

If Brook's assertion that interactivity is present in all shows across all genres is accurate, then the significance of interaction becomes greatly undermined. However, it could be argued that Brook's audience is of a different agency to those found in immersive theatre: there is a greater expectation of immediacy within immersive performance theatregoers. Perhaps interaction holds more importance here, leading to the question of whether interaction is included, or exaggerated, in immersive theatre pieces simply to fulfil a participant's expectation. To avoid the suggestion that the Micro-Scene is using interaction for interactivity's sake, 9/11 focused on immersive design rather than contrived interaction opportunities. The interactivity evident through conversing with characters, and through being immersed in another world was a welcome, but incidental, element created in the journey towards presenting that immersible environment: a by-product of immersive theatre.

Conclusions

The success of the Micro-Scene must first be judged against the questions raised during the planning phase, and during process of making each decision.

Throughout the process, I was constantly referring to Devine's concept of the 'other world'. This offered drive and focus for the project, but also created problems. The desire to create illusionistic scenery in the street zone led to a desire to create an almost-first-hand emotional experience of being there. By this, I mean that I intended to test the idea that the Micro-Scene can offer participants as much of a sense of actually being there as possible. The caveat, 'almost' came from the recognition that a show that portrays an historical event can never be truly 'first-hand', as the event has been and gone. It is therefore important to define this idea: there is a commitment to offering audiences as close an experience as possible, across multiple senses. From participants' arrival into the theatre foyer, through to the move out of the street zone, audiences were treated as though they were visitors to New York on September 11th 2001. The background nature of the 'live' news programmes set the tone for a normal day, giving the sense that as a normal day, life will go on whether the audience are paying attention or not. Participants' time in the street scene offered all major senses an opportunity to receive information about what it would have been like to be there: they could see how normality had been destroyed by the rubble, dust and broken glass; they could hear the chaos and panic; they could smell and taste the dust and ash in the air; they could feel the different textured materials - brick, sandstone, glass, concrete dust - both in their hand and underfoot. In this sense, the Micro-Scene did offer an 'almost first-hand experience'.

However, there was no genuine sense of fear, shock or panic amongst participants, as there was amongst bystanders at the original attack, and why would there be: participants knew they were safe? When participants looked up beyond the tops of the flats, they could see the buildings suddenly stop, with no sky above. The thick haze and smoke did mask the theatre infrastructure; the truss and pipework for example, but this served more to render the unreal elements invisible rather than to create more 'real' street. In considering these flaws, areas of the Micro-Scene did not provide a first-hand experience - even by the lower thresholds of theatrical standards.

Despite these flaws, however, audiences knew they were attending a piece of theatre, and were assumed to have suspended their disbelief somewhat. In placing participants into the action, and so close to displays of grief and fear, most reported a powerful sympathy towards the characters, really believing their stories. During several performances, when the young man on the phone had just seen his girlfriend fall from a high floor and fell, sobbing, to his knees, participants approached him and tried to comfort him. One helped him to his feet and tried to help him evacuate the area when the time came to do so. It may well be that these participants were empathising by proxy with the real people at the real-world event, but either way, there was a deep engagement from some participants, suggesting that the feeling of actually being there, and being involved, was powerful.

Overall, on the question of whether a Micro-Scene can provide a close emotional experience of a global event, it is impossible to give an incontrovertible answer. The 9/11 experiment proved that it is possible to create the 'almost first-hand' experience, but that experience was patchy during this process: by placing the outdoors indoors, a Micro-Scene will detract from the true sense of being there; the knowledge that everyone is safe, and that the city does recover from the attack will prevent those feelings of fear from creating the first-hand experience fully.

In the quest to create an 'other world' for participants to step into, problems were not limited to the participants' knowledge of the event's end result, or their assured safety. The degree of realism created incompatibilities on many levels. On one hand, 9/11 aimed to engage participants in a world not of their own, and if doing so completely faithfully, should have provided an outdoor lot, with authentic, life-sized buildings and street paraphernalia. The fundamental clash here was with budget and resources. The presented set was small, indoors, and though using real elements (e.g. bricks, glass, sandstone and fire); most of what was presented was not real (e.g. canvas flats, cyclorama, theatre lighting and projected images). There was a spectrum within the unreal elements, with the cat-litter dust not being immediately apparent as false, but the black drapes and wall being clearly not of the world being represented. However, even if there was a large enough budget to provide authentic scenery, participants will still know they are there to experience theatre: realism will not fool audiences into believing they are in another world. It is unfortunate that this observation was not considered earlier. 9/11 bounced between attempting to create authentic New York, and using theatrical conventions to fill gaps. It was a desire to provide an immersive environment that clashed with the low budget and inadequacies of the available actors, resulting in a confused notion of what kind of illusion the Micro-Scene attempted to create.

The question of whether actors should be used at all was considered early on. The primary aim of the project was to discover whether theatrical technologies can drive an immersive experience. 9/11 did suggest that it was possible for technology alone to carry the story. However, the section that relied totally on technology to do so (the firefighters' story) was stodgy. Had this section toned down the use of projection, and relied more on the soundscape and exploration of the set, it may have been more successful. But as a milestone assessment, 9/11 as a public performance did not provide a strong argument for removing actors altogether.

The element of 9/11 that did indicate a necessity for actors, whilst still retaining the status of theatre technologies, was the section with the dorm girls. Notwithstanding the limited opportunity for interacting with the audience that needs further work, this section succeeded in showing that actors are a key requirement for linking participants into the created, 'real' world. By operating the camcorder, and contextualising the scenery around them, the girls didn't so much create and progress a narrative, but rather offered explanations and alternative explanations for the 'other world' that participants found themselves in. They were able to apply a human impact to all the events around them, leading to more links through which audiences could form their all-important emotional responses. Technology lacks this human element, meaning that whilst it can evoke strong emotions and opinions, it is very difficult for technology to adapt to audience engagement and response dynamically, and to therefore provide different stimuli night after night. However useful the actors were in bringing the technology seamlessly into the 'other world', the reference to Gröppel-Wegener's observation earlier in this paper - that one can never truly recreate a historical event with actors - rings loud here: there was always the spectre of unrealism hanging over the use of actors in 9/11; this diverted attention away from what the production could have become.

Actors were therefore used as extensions of the location, of the set, rather than elements within their own right. They existed in that world because the location expects them to be there - they are to be treated as living scenery. 9/11 failed to meet this point in the section of the young man on the phone, as his inclusion was not balanced within the mise-en-scène. However, he depicted a real person in a real tragic situation, and acted genuinely given the circumstances: oblivious to his surroundings and focused only on himself and his tragedy. Many participants reported this section as being the most emotionally stimulating to experience. This monologue did strengthen engagement for many, immersing them deeper in this 'other world' as well as forging new responses internally. It is interesting to note that in a project that aimed to promote technology as a primary stimulus, it was an actor who excepted this rule that got the most vocal response.

In speaking more generally about the Micro-Scene, actors aren't a necessity as it depends on the piece, but they are an important consideration if the self-styled genre is to distinguish itself from static installation. For all the reasons supporting the use of actors in 9/11, it is important to observe the impact of scenography as a separate entity. The set alone provided participants with a clear sense of destruction, with the road signs, posters and paraphernalia inside the deli giving clues as to the New York location. Any participants with geographical knowledge of New York City could even place themselves within a few streets of the World Trade Centre site, based on the street names used in the set. The timing of their placement within the set is also detectable from the amount of debris and smouldering papers. When the front of house and deli videos are taken into consideration, the location and time becomes very clear, and audiences have followed a substantial section of the narrative already, using only visual media and set. The lighting and smoke help to create an eerie atmosphere, as the daylight is partially blocked by the clouds of dust in the air, but do not progress any narrative strands, beyond the snapshot in time. An exception to this in the lighting department is the use of the traffic lights, which continue to cycle through their phases despite the absence of traffic: the juxtaposition of normal life carrying on unobserved amidst all the destruction, as well as an indicator of the continuation of time.

Two of the three narrative angles relied on actors to drive them, with the young man on the phone limited to his mobile phone prop as his only interaction with theatrical technology (besides being lit). This narrative strand failed in its attempt to rely on theatrical technologies, though it did bring participants' focus to a different part of the set. However, the dorm girls' narrative strand did use technology to drive the narrative, with the video recording on the handheld camera a key point of their section: these actors existed mainly to link this technology to the world of the street scene. The firefighters' story strand relied totally on theatrical technology to drive it. Sound, lighting and visual media were all utilised, with the intention to remove audience from the New York world, and to bring them into a state of reflection - in preparation for entering the reflective zone. Originally, the firefighters' story was to be told solely through the soundscape. The projection was added as another point of reference, 'something to do' whilst participants listened. It was intended that the audience can dip in and out of either the visual story or the aural story. The overall intention of the firefighters' story being presented in a stylised, theatrical method was to dislocate audiences from the world of the New York street. However, in the final performances the projection was too static and lengthy, making audiences believe they were expected to stand and focus on it. Ultimately, this section dislocated too much from what had gone before, whilst perhaps a more passive projection, and brighter (but still stylised) lighting would make this change in style less jarring. However, a substantial portion of 9/11 did provide both narrative drive and immersive experience either exclusively through theatrical technology, or with actors playing the supporting role to technology. It was one key technological section that failed to maintain a strong engagement with participants. It could be argued that it is a case of refining, rather than replacing the firefighters' story with actors, that would improve this.

9/11 set out to create an immersive environment, not necessarily an interactive one. What was discovered through this aim was that, in order to provide audiences with a world they can engage in, it must include the same interactive elements as the original world being represented. If you were to walk down a street in New York after the towers had been hit, you would encounter other people and have the choice on how much interaction, if any, to have with them; you would have the choice on what to touch, including dynamically risk assessing the elements to touch or pick up. So in order to provide any kind of robust immersion, realism must be an objective (albeit the magnitude of realism is variable), and with realism comes the need to provide inherent interactivity. 9/11 provided interaction for participants, but it was a by-product of the desire to immerse them into the environment, rather than a distinct objective. For each performance, it was the job of each actor, but in particular the two dorm girls, to encourage participants to interact. By encouraging interaction, implied permission was granted to interact with the world around them, and thus promote the illusion of free will - a concept I borrowed from Alan Lane (discussed earlier). The nature of 9/11 meant that every performance and audience were very different in how they interacted. In some shows, there were lots of questions and responses, with the desired two-way conversation achieved. Other participants were very quiet and did not engage in conversation - leading to the question of whether interaction with actors was in fact stifling the immersive experience. The actors were simply not of a high enough standard to be able to cope with totally natural interactions with participants, by improvising in role. It perhaps would have been helpful to them to limit the experience to one participant at a time, or to fill the space with many bystander characters, with simultaneous action taking the spotlight off any one actor at any one time. Interaction between audience and set was subtle and natural, limited to passive sensory interactions: feeling the debris underfoot; hearing the crunch of glass broken underfoot; and feeling the roughness of sandstone or brick. This subtle interaction provides the Micro-Scene with a gentle level of immersion to participants, though it is recognised that such passive immersion techniques are not limited to the Micro-Scene - they are evident in a range of both theatrical and non-theatrical immersive design projects.

Interaction must take place in any show - to limit it simply isn't theatre. Even in a West End musical, the energy from the stage is significantly reliant on the reactions from the audience: think of how many times a theatre practitioner has heard an actor complain of a 'dead' audience, or exit the first scene with an anticipatory smile as he proclaims 'a good audience'. This point reinforces the premise that 9/11 discovered: that interaction will happen by accident in any show. In the Micro-Scene experiment, this was found to be even truer when immersive theatre is the style. The Micro-Scene does not need to focus on interaction in order to engage its audience: in immersive design, interaction will naturally occur as an indicator of engagement rather than as a precursor to it.

9/11 is merely one milestone in a long learning process. I am pleased with how the narrative was structured, and how it progressed through a 'real' timeline. The set, lighting and soundscape had the desired effect when audiences entered the street scene - for the majority who had not seen the environment before the show, there was a 'wow' factor of walking into such a detailed and encompassing set. The stimulation of all senses worked well, with touch and smell seemingly unexpected by most participants.

Looking specifically at each production element against the backdrop of immersive design, the success of the Micro-Scene from a technical perspective is mixed. The set was confusing. In one sense, the use of textured floor materials drew directly from Devine's 'other world' concept, creating a level of detail that held attention and conveyed information about the scene. The wide range of appropriate materials in the pile of rubble, the 'working' traffic lights, and the feel of the sandstone and bricks on the two buildings, also added to the encouragement of exploration within this zone. However, this level of detail was not consistent: the large expanses of black, though used deliberately, did not match the style of illusionistic scenery offered by the floor and brick walls. The tops of the buildings were visible, leaving a gap between the street scene and the grid above, and the deli windows allowed partial glimpses of the fact that the building was made from canvas flats. These lapses in detailed illusion caused the confusion: the set was neither a successful 'other world' of complete immersion, nor was it a minimalist symbolism that the black surfaces hinted towards becoming. Ultimately, this mis-match of styles was enforced by lack of budget - prompting consideration of whether my intentions should have been pursued at all under such circumstances. If 9/11 was to be produced again in an ideal world, I would aim to carry the detail and multi-layered approach throughout the entirety of the street. The explorable world would be expanded, as per the original plans, to include the interior of the deli, and detail extended to, and through, the grid. Participants would enter the street via the deli, and would exit into the reflective zone through another building - maintaining the illusion of the 'other world' throughout the entirety of this zone. Further research into the use of fibre-reinforced plastic and concrete (as used in large, outdoor theme park sets) to create highly realistic buildings would be required, in order to extend the detail of the bricks to the whole structure without simply constructing a real building.

Lighting was simple and successful. Combining the established methods of Jackie Staines, Stanley McCandless and Francis Reid, a naturalistic state was created that fitted in with the illusion of time and location being presented. Whilst the lighting was not a realistic representation of daylight outdoors, it has been established earlier in the discussion that participants will never forget that they are in a theatre. Thus, a suspension of disbelief was assumed, and the lighting matched the convention for representing daylight within theatre. The traffic light set was influenced by my own use of practical lighting sources whilst working in commercial theatre. This observed practice added a useful sense of time to the street zone, also providing a contrast between normality and disaster whilst retaining the illusion of being in a street. Another feature of the lighting design that drew on my experience in commercial theatre, was the change from naturalistic lighting to the stylised, dark state used for the firefighters' story. Both the nature of the change and the state itself were influenced by musical theatre; used as a device to reinforce theatricality rather than the illusion of naturalism. The montage of radio transmissions was not of the time and location of the preceding illusion, and the lighting state reflected this change successfully.

The visual media successfully reflected the suggestions of practitioners such as Julia Bardsley, David Barbour and Wendall Harrington at times, though at others went directly against theories of others discussed in this paper. Earlier, I discussed the three practitioners' wish to avoid having visual imaging overshadow a performance. Bardsley was concerned with the medium of screen, Barbour with the scale, and Harrington with the unnecessary inclusion of visual imagery. In the front of house zone, the video shown on the wall-mounted televisions was unimposing: the fact that it began as regular, mundane morning television was in line with the desire not to force unnecessary content upon participants. The television in the deli was small and appropriately included - its scale could not be accused of overshadowing the rest of the experience, and the diegetic nature of it did not detract from the environment. However, Bardsley's deliberate attempt to avoid the white screen at the back of the space was conspicuously ignored in 9/11. The use of a white cyclorama on which the continuance of the physical set was projected was not as "tyrannical" as Bardsley had feared, as it was well masked by smoke and rubble, and so was not glaringly bright or overpowering. However, it clearly stood out from the rest of the black or stone-effect surroundings. Even though the image blended in relatively well with the hazy lighting state in front of it, there was no illusion that this was anything other than a white cloth. Further research into opaque dark screens (as opposed to the gauze that was tried out in the planning process) and wrap-around LED screens would be ideal, although I acknowledge the latter would command a large budget. There can be no question on the outcome of the firefighters' story projections, however: this projection did not work. It was long and static, and drew attention to a large expanse of black wall intended to encourage individual imagination, instead encouraging thoughts of what was missing. With an improved budget, this black area would have been covered with further scenic detail, though I am pleased with how the principle of the 'blank canvas' worked at the ends of the space. The projected text and video, if included at all, could have been split into multiple locations across the set, providing a 360 degree 'screen', utilising elements of set.

Sound was split into two areas: technical sound design; and conceptual sound design. Though utilising multiple sound sources that required a not inconsiderable amount of planning and set-up, the result for participants was mostly subtle. Drawing on John Leonard's method of building a layered soundscape, participants entered into a scene that gently gave audiences real audio from the event without forcing it upon them, or requiring total concentration. When participants were gently pushed towards concentrating on a single element, sound cues made this clear: the lowering of the general soundscape level and the raising of the firefighters' radio transmissions level supported the overall departure from the illusion of the street at a specific time, into a more stylised summary of one angle of the event. Technically, the design was complex relative to the size of space, and duration and content of Micro-Scene. Different speaker positions enabled the effects of distance and immersion to be played with, though the absence of scenery on one side of the space meant that the sound was not truly surrounding participants, merely operating as a form of horseshoe-shaped array instead. Artistically, there was enough detail and layering to stand up to scrutiny. Subtlety and accuracy in audio used reinforced the idea of 'being there' - although the differences in acoustic quality between digitally reproduced sound and live sound were as clear as they are in any theatre: further research opportunities lie in the area of closing this gap;

audiences know the difference between live and replayed audio, and so the question in future is whether entire soundscapes can be created live, and still retain the depth of detail and accuracy that the replayed audio gives, or whether the technology can be improved to the point where the human ear cannot distinguish between live and reproduced sound.

The presentation style brought by the actors was not perfect: at times the acting was not natural, as actors with no experience of immersive theatre reverted to what they knew, and began closing out their co-characters (the participants), trying to perform for them rather than with them. If the opportunity arose to recreate 9/11, I would allow much more time for participants to explore the environment on their own or with the people they arrived with. This would retain the use of characters in the scene, but instead would experiment with the addition of many more actors: a street teeming with bystanders, survivors and rescuers, whose individual stories and interactions continue simultaneously, in real time, with participants free to intersperse and observe and interact with whomever they wish, in whatever order they wish. This would take Alan Lane and Michael Devine's idea of what immersive design is, extending it to the very structure of the performance, rather than simply the mise-en-scène.

Looking laterally at immersive design concepts throughout this research, it is interesting to note that there are many similarities between the Micro-Scene as defined in the 9/11 project, and museum theatre. Though the intention at the beginning of this phase of research was to site the experiment within the field of immersive theatre, I am surprised to have found further avenues to explore in a museum context. Perhaps it is the close links between a desire to educate in the museum, and the desire, or even obligation, to educate within the school that housed 9/11 that forms a false resemblance. Or perhaps the subject matter - based on a recent, though still historical, event that drew so much interest from so many people - presented in a learning environment skewed the style towards education. In any case, the similarities between the use of multi-sensory environments, actors and fact-based participatory theatre in both museum theatre and

9/11 asks a question about whether the 'other world' immersive design methods explored here can be successfully applied to an educational theatre setting. It is a question that I did not set out to explore with this project, but it is a question that, with the other technological and process questions that remain unanswered above, provide opportunity for further research.

References

•Ayckbourn, A 2012, 'Absent Friends', Directed by Jeremy Herrin [Harold Pinter theatre, 02/03/12]

•Barbour, D 2011, 'The Prevalence of Projections', American Theatre, 28, 10, pp. 28-32, International Bibliography of Theatre & Dance with Full Text, EBSCOhost, viewed 3 June 2012

•Bay-Cheng, S Kattenbelt, C Lavender, A 2011, 'Mapping Intermediality in Performance', Amsterdam: Amsterdam University Press

•Billington, M 2012, 'Absent Friends - Review', [online] Guardian Newspaper, Available at http://www.guardian.co.uk/ stage/2012/feb/10/absent-friends-review [Accessed 20/06/12]

•Brown, R 2010, 'Sound: A Reader in Theatre Practice', Basingstoke: Palgrave Macmillan

•Coney 2012, 'A small town anywhere' [online], Coney Theatre Company website, Available at http://www.youhavefoundconey.net/2012/01/21/a-small-town-anywhere-2/ [Accessed 27/05/12]

•Coveney, M 2010, 'Stage Directions: immersive theatre' [online] Prospect Magazine, Available at http://www.prospectmagazine.co.uk/magazine/you-me-bum-bum-train-one-on-one-theatre/ [Accessed 25/04/12]

•Dietrich, R 1989, 'Modern British and Irish Drama 1890 to 1950: A Critical History' (revised online version) [online], available at http://chuma.cas.usf.edu/~dietrich/britishdrama.htm [Accessed 07/10/12]

•Gardner, L 2010, 'Immersive theatre: take us to the edge, but don't throw us in', Guardian Newspaper [online], Available at http://www.guardian.co.uk/stage/theatreblog/2010/apr/07/immersive-theatre-terrifying-experience [Accessed 21/05/12]

•Grainger, R 2010, 'Suspending Disbelief: Theatre as Context for Sharing', Eastbourne: Sussex Academic Press

•Gröppel-Wegener, A 2011, 'Creating Experiences Through Architecture'. *In* Jackson, A & Kidd, J (eds.), 'Performing Heritage', chapter 3, Manchester: Manchester University Press

•Hickling, A 2009, 'They Only Come At Night: Resurrections - Review', Guardian Newspaper, Stage section [online], Available at http://www.guardian.co.uk/stage/2009/sep/08/they-only-come-night-resurrection [Accessed 20/05/12]

•Higgins, C 2009, 'Immersive Theatre - Tired and Hackneyed Already?', Guardian Newspaper, Culture section [online], Available at http://www.guardian.co.uk/culture/charlottehigginsblog/2009/dec/07/theatre-punchdrunk [Accessed 20/05/12]

•Howard, P 2009, 'What is Scenography', Oxford: Routledge

•Izzo, G 1997, 'The Art of Play: The New Genre of Interactive Theatre', Portsmouth NH: Heinemann

•Johnson, D 2010, 'The Skin of the Theatre: an Interview with Julia Bardsley' [Word document - online] Queen Mary, University of London College Publications, Available at https://qmro.qmul.ac.uk/xmlui/handle/123456789/2102?show=full [accessed 27/04/12]

•Jones, A 2008, 'Artaud and Strasberg a Quest for Reality', [ebook], Available at http://www.amazon.com/Artaud-Strasberg-Quest-Reality-Jones/dp/1409229688/ref=sr_1_1?s=books&ie=UTF8&qid=1350705780&sr=1-1&keywords=1409229688 [Accessed 18/10/12]

•Kabakov, I & E 2012, 'The Red Wagon' [online], Ilya & Emilia Kabakov's official website, Available at http://www.ilya-emilia-kabakov.com/index.php/installations/the-red-wagon/interactive-installation [Accessed 01/06/12]

•Lacey, S 1995, 'British Realist Theatre: The New Wave in its Context 1956-1965', London: Routledge

•Lane, A 2009, 'Alan Lane on Slung Low and They Only Come Out at Night' [online], London Theatre Blog, Available at http://www.londontheatreblog.co.uk/alan-lane-on-slung-low-and-they-only-come-out-at-night/ [Accessed 20/05/12]

•Leonard, J 2002, 'Theatre Sound', London: Routledge

•Ludwig, F 2011, 'Theatre Minds in Immersive Design', TD&T: Theatre Design & Technology, 47, 1, pp. 49-58, International Bibliography of Theatre & Dance with Full Text, EBSCOhost, viewed 20 May 2012.

•Moore, K 1997, 'Museums and Popular Culture', London: Cassell

•Nelson, R 2006, 'Practice-as-research and the Problem of Knowledge', Performance Research: A Journal of the Performing Arts, 11 (4), 105-116

•Reid, F 2002, 'The Stage Lighting Handbook', London: Routledge

•Schumacher, C 1996 ed., 'Naturalism and Symbolism in European Theatre', Cambridge University Press

•Sexton, J 2010, Defining "Scene" to simplify and strengthen your improv, [online] Fusebox Theatre Company, Available at http://www.fuseboxtheatre.com/defining-scene-to-strengthen-and-simplify-your-improv/ [Accessed 24/04/12]

•Slung Low 2009, 'They Only Come at Night: Resurrections', Directed by Alan Lane [Lowry].

•Staines, J 2000, 'Lighting Techniques for Theatre In The Round', Entertainment Technology Press

•Tolkoff, E 1995, 'Actors bring exhibits to life', Back Stage, 36, 44, p. 30, Business Source Complete, EBSCOhost, viewed 14 February 2013.

•Trumbull, E 2009, 'Realism', [online] Northern Virginia Community College website, Available at http://novaonline.nvcc.edu/eli/spd130et/realism.htm [Accessed 19/06/12]

•Zuk, P 2006, 'Raymond Deane' Dublin:
Field Day Books

Bibliography - further reading

• Baugh, C (2005), 'Theatre Performance and Technology: The Development of Scenography in the Twentieth Century' Basingstoke: Palgrave Macmillan

•Belt Up Theatre (2009), Immersive Theatre Already Over? Certainly Not! [online] Available at: http://beltuptheatre.blogspot.sg/2009/12/immersive-theatre-already-over.html [Accessed 13/09/11]

• Billington, M (2009), Theatre Review: Kursk [online] Available at: http://www.guardian.co.uk/stage/2009/jun/09/kursk-young-vic [Accessed 25/04/12]

• Bridal, T (2004), 'Exploring Museum Theatre' Plymouth: Rowman

• Collins, J & Nisbet, A (eds.)(2010), 'Theatre and Performance Design: A Reader in Scenography' Abingdon: Routledge

•Gardner, L (2007), We Make Our Own Ghosts Here [online] Available at: http://m.guardian.co.uk/stage/2007/sep/12/theatre.edgarallanpoe?cat=stage&type=article [Accessed 01/09/11]

•Gompertz, W (2010), Immersive Theatre Meets Opera [online] Available at: http://www.bbc.co.uk/blogs/thereporters/willgompertz/2010/07/immersive_theatre_meets_opera.html [Accessed 21/10/11]

•Guardian (n.d.), Punchdrunk Guardian Page [online repository] Available at: http://www.guardian.co.uk/stage/punchdrunk [Accessed 28/08/11]

• Howdon, C (2009), Beyond the Front Line - Lowry Theatre Salford [online] Available at: http://www.thepublicreviews.com/beyond-the-front-line-lowry-theatre-salford/ [Accessed 23/09/11]

• Ideas Tap (2011a), Upstaged: Immersive Theatre [online] Available at: http://www.ideastap.com/ideasmag/all-articles/upstaged-immersive-theatre [Accessed 12/12/11]

• Ideas Tap (2011b), Immersive Theatre: Yay or Nay? [online] Available at: http://www.ideastap.com/IdeasMag/all-articles/immersive-theatre-belt-up [Accessed 03/03/12]

• Jackson, A (ed.) (2002), 'Learning Through Theatre' London: Taylor and Francis

• Jackson, A (2007), 'Theatre, Education and the Making of Meanings: Art or Instrument' Manchester: Manchester University Press

• Mitchell, B (n.d.), Immersive Installation Arts [online - artist's official website] Available at: http://immersiveinstallationart.com [Accessed 31/08/11]

• Oddey, A & White, C (eds.)(2006), 'The Potentials of Spaces: The Theory and Practice of Scenography and Performance' Bristol: Intellect

• Sky (2011), Video: Sky Arts At Headlong Theatre's Decade [online video of broadcast programme] Available at: http://skyarts.sky.com/sky-arts-at-headlong-theatres-decade-video [Accessed 26/02/13]

• Wooster, R (2007), 'Contemporary Theatre in Education', Bristol: Intellect

Appendices

Note on appendices:

The following pages present all those appendices that are either still image or text. Audio and Video appendices are to be found at this online location

http://sdrv.ms/S4l9X7

If there is a problem with this link, please email the author at kieran@kpburgess.com to arrange alternative delivery.

Within this location, appendices are split into two folders within an Appendices folder; Audio and Video. Filenames within these two folders reflect the appendix letter referred to within the body of this thesis, along with a brief description. For example, 'Video Appendix D' can be found at the above link, in \Appendices\Video\Video Appendix D - whole show

Appendix A - Reflective Zone
'Wordle'

Appendix C - First proposal for the audience's journey through Micro-Scene

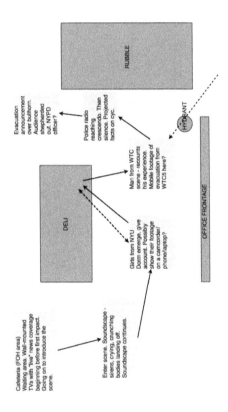

Appendix D - Second draft of Audience Navigation

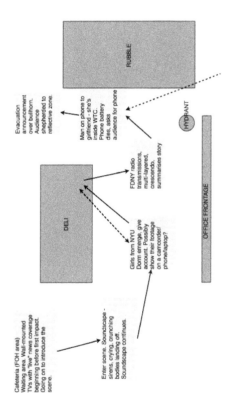

Appendix E - Final draft showing audience navigation through Micro-Scene

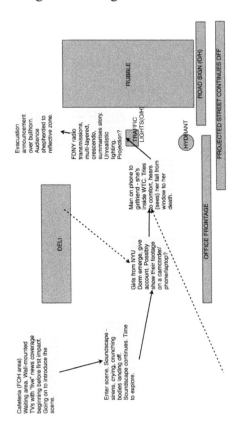

RUBBLE

ROAD SIGN (OH)

PROJECTED STREET CONTINUES OFF

TRAFFIC LIGHTS/OH

HYDRANT

OFFICE FRONTAGE

DELI

Evacuation announcement over bullhorn. Audience shepherded to reflective zone.

FDNY radio transmissions, multi-layered, crescendo, summarises story. Unrealistic lighting. Projection?

Man on phone to girlfriend – she's inside WTC. Tries to comfort, hears (sees) her fall from window to her death.

Girls from NYU Dorm emerge, give account. Possibly show their footage on a camcorder/ phone/laptop?

Cafeteria (FOH area) Waiting area. Wall-mounted TVs with "live" news coverage beginning before first impact. Going on to introduce the scene.

Enter scene. Soundscape - sirens, crying, crunching bodies landing off. Soundscape continues. Time to explore.

Appendix F - Lighting Plan

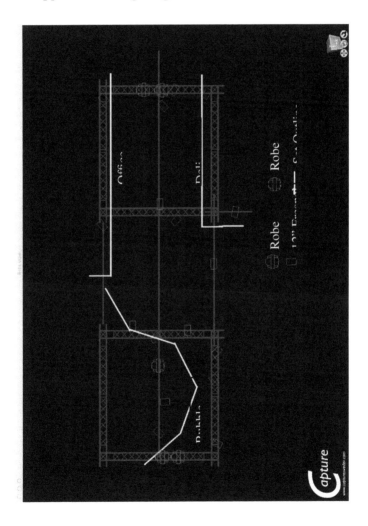

Appendix G - Sound Schematic Diagram

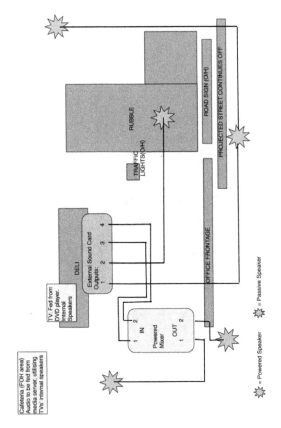

Appendix H - Sound 'Q' List (first draft, used for creation of soundscapes and effects)

Q no	When	Type	Description
0.5	Preset	Audio	Soundscape: mixed sirens, walkie-talkie bursts, shouting (New York accents/ indistinguishable?), chatter, from output 1. Chatter, random smoke alarms and evacuation alarms from multiple buildings, occasional siren from output 3.

| 1 | Audience enter | Audio | Long-running track (20 min? This can be a loop) of sporadic loud, horrific crunches of bodies hitting concrete from great height, of bodies crashing through canopy roofs and glass, bodies hitting cars etc. Gaps of a minute or two give or take between each hit is good. This will cut through the soundscape, running over the top. Output 1 only |
| 2 | Dorm Girls play video | Level Down Audio | Slow, 10s? lev down of Q0.5. Q1 unaffected? Audio from NYU Dorm Girls Video - out of output 1 and 3 - reinforcement volume only. Unnatural (non-diegetic). |

| 3 | After Dorm Girls Video, interrupt dialogue | Audio

Fade and Stop | Walkie-Talkie chatter from Fire Dept. A montage of edited clips to tell the story of the firefighters. To include (ideally) those en route, those reporting back visible flames etc, those within building, those sending civilians for medical attention, those who are panicking and scared, those who cannot be reached and those who we don't hear from again. This is only a guide. To begin with, this will need to punch through at a good volume from output 2 only.
F&S Q1 simultaneously. |

3.5	Auto - 15s or so after start of Q3	Output change (level up) Fade and Stop	Fade up Q3 audio on output 1 and 3, to provide a cinematic, non-natural experience. F&S Q0.5 simultaneously
4	End of firefighters story track	Audio	Resume/restart Q0.5 and Q1 with appropriate outputs
5	7s after end of male on phone's conversation	Audio	Loud crunch of body hitting ground. Output 1.
6	30s after 'male on phone' has hung up	Audio Fade and Stop	Low, ominous rumbling/ creaking, loud! Bullhorn announcement repeating order to evacuate the area (NY accent) from output 1 F&S Q4 simultaneously

Appendix I - Detailed description of the facilities and equipment available for *9/11*

In addition to the 10 metre x 5 metre (approx.) playing space, there is further space behind a fixed cyclorama hanging point, but this is roughly triangular and has a solid wall running down the centre. This space would become useful for operating technologies from. The main playing space houses a truss on chain hoists, capable of flying into the deck. The truss is equipped with eight socapex outlets, giving 48 channels of dimmable power, as well as a number of DMX outlets. A large quantity of audio and data tie lines connect either side of the stage (across the 10 metre axis), on facilities panels that also offer cue light ties, communications headset ties, clean 13 amp power, 16 amp power and 12 further channels of dimmable power via socapex.

Eight hanging points for masking legs were available, as well as a cyclorama and a set of full black drapes on a tab track. Eight Robe moving lights were available - four Colour Wash 575 and four Colour Spot 575, along with a number of Chroma-Q Colour Punch LED fixtures and a large stock of 1.2 kilowatt Fresnels and Profiles, and a large stock of parcans and floods. The separated space that houses the retractable raked bleacher seating also contains a truss on chain hoists, with a further 60 dimmable channels of power via socapex, and data outlets spread around the whole unit. A Jands Vista T4 lighting desk and an ETC Congo lighting desk were available, as well as a full PA system including racked amps, passive loudspeakers, subwoofers, powered monitor speakers, a Soundcraft GB8 40 channel analogue mixer and a Yamaha LS9 32 channel digital mixer. A number of computers were made available, some of which included Show Control Software (by Mike Daniell) and external sound cards, and access to the building's digital signage servers feeding media to wall-mounted televisions in the front of house area.

Audio Appendix D
'Evacuate The Area' sound cue. Found at http://sdrv.ms/S4l9X7 then \Appendices\Audio\Audio Appendix D - evacuate the area.wav

Video Appendix A
'FOH 1' - the 'live' morning news programme from September 11, 2001, that played in the Front of House area while participants arrived and waited to enter the street scene. Found at http://sdrv.ms/S4l9X7 then \Appendices\Video\Video Appendix A - FOH 1.m4v

Video Appendix B
'FOH 2' - the 'live' morning news programme from September 11, 2001, that played in the corridor between Front of House foyer and the street scene, showing the first tower collapse. Found at **http://sdrv.ms/S4l9X7** then \Appendices\Video\Video Appendix B - FOH 2.m4v

Video Appendix C
'Dorm Girls' - the footage captured by the two university students from their apartment. As shown in the street scene via a handheld video camera playback screen. Found at **http://sdrv.ms/S4l9X7** then \Appendices\Video\Video Appendix C - Dorm Girls.mov

Video Appendix D
'Whole show' - POV footage from a participant as he moves from the corridor (immediately after the FOH 2 video of the tower collapse) into the street scene, and then through to the reflective zone. Found at

http://sdrv.ms/S4l9X7 then
\Appendices\Video\Video Appendix D -
whole show.mov

CPSIA information can be obtained
at www.ICGtesting.com
Printed in the USA
LVHW081413091222
734855LV00012B/287